Tough Plants
for
FLORIDA GARDENS

Low Care, No Care, Tried and True Winners

Published by Cool Springs Press, 101 Forrest Crossing Boulevard, Suite 100, Franklin, Tennessee 37064

Rushing, Felder, 1952-
    Tough plants for Florida gardens : low care, no care, tried and true
    winners / Felder Rushing.
       p. cm.
    ISBN 1-5918-6120-9
    Includes bibliographical references and index.
    1. Landscape plants—Florida. 2. Low maintenance gardening—Florida.
    I. Title.
SB407.R874 2004
635.9'09759--dc22
                                    2004025083

First printing 2004
Printed in the United States of America
10 9 8 7 6 5 4 3 2

Managing Editor: Jenny Andrews
Cover Design: Becky Brawner, Unlikely Suburban Design
Production Artist: S.E. Anderson

Visit the Cool Springs Press website at **www.coolspringspress.net**.

Tough Plants

for

FLORIDA GARDENS

Low Care, No Care, Tried and True Winners

Felder Rushing

COOL SPRINGS PRESS

Franklin, Tennessee

Dedication:

I dedicate this book to the long-suffering horticulture staffs of Florida's public and private botanic gardens and state parks, who calmly handle hurricanes, giant grass-hoppers, and tourists; and to the thousands of Master Gardener volunteers who quite often are so helpful and friendly it can make you want to scream!

Acknowledgements:

I'm really serious here—this book would be neither possible nor practical if not for the insights and experience of the following hard-core horticulture professionals, all "real gardeners" who in one important way or another helped compile and tweak the list of plants, took extra time to take me exploring gardens throughout Florida, shared their hard-earned notes, and argued with me (usually winning), sometimes late into the night, over plants and misconceptions about what it takes to be a gardener in the Sunshine, Rain, Sand, and Hurricane State:

Alan and Ellen Shapiro, owners, Grandiflora, Gainesville; Beth Weidner, Manager, Alfred MacClay Gardens State Park, Tallahassee; Cass Meadows, aquatic plant specialist, Indian River Lily Company, Vero Beach; Edward Gilman, Associate Professor of Horticulture, University of Florida, Gainesville; Gene Joyner, Palm Beach County Extension Horticulturist, West Palm Beach; Georgia Tasker, Master Gardener and *Miami Herald* garden columnist, Coconut Grove; Jan Abernathie, botanist, Caribbean Gardens, Naples; Kent Schwartz, graduate horticulturist and landscape maintenance, Pensacola; Linda Bell, Master Gardener extraordinaire, Tampa; Randy Harelson, owner, The Gourd Garden, Sea Grove; Rick Brown, nurseryman (and Sydney's fun loving husband), Riverview; Rick Schoellhorn, University of Florida Floriculture Specialist, Gainesville; Stephen and Kristen Pategas, Hortus Oasis Designs, Winter Park; Sydney Park Brown, Hillsborough County Extension Agent, Seffner; Tom MacCubbin, Orange County Extension Horticulturist, Orlando; Wayne McGonegal, Horticulture Instructor, Disney Institute, Orlando.

I especially want to honor the insights, guidance, flexibility, patience (most of the time), and good cheer of Jenny Andrews, my long-suffering editor at Cool Springs Press. She has earned a special crown in Heaven. Her boss Hank McBride has been a real trusting gem and supporter as well.

In addition to cruising dozens of cemeteries and back streets of small towns from the Panhandle to the Keys, along both the Atlantic coast and the Gulf of Mexico, I spent countless hours photographing and studying plants, and interviewing curators, of the following gardens:

Fairchild Tropical Gardens, near Miami; Harry P. Leu Gardens, Orlando; Bok Tower Gardens, Lake Wales; Bellingrath Home and Gardens near Mobile, Alabama; Kanapaha Botanical Gardens, Gainesville; Marie Selby Botanical Gardens, Sarasota; Mounts Botanical Garden, West Palm Beach; Audubon House and Tropical Gardens, Key West; Flamingo Gardens, near Ft. Lauderdale; Montgomery Botanical Center, Coral Gables; Alfred MacClay State Park, Tallahassee; Florida House Learning Center, Sarasota; Extension Demonstration Garden, Fort Pierce; Caribbean Gardens, Naples; and the cycad collection at Disney's Wild Animal Kingdom, Orlando. Oh, and of course the Coral Castle in Homestead.

Table of Contents

Foreword

I wish I had owned this book years ago when I started my nursery in Florida. I had grown up in Louisiana gardening in Mississippi River delta soil, possibly the richest, blackest soil on the planet. After college I moved to southern New England, and immediately started a garden. Rhode Island's temperate four-season climate spoiled me: peonies grow effortlessly, and your knees and back get a yearly winter vacation. When I moved to Florida (arriving on the same day Hurricane Andrew roared through the peninsula) I brought the usual enthusiasm of a new transplant: Life will be grand. Every plant will grow. Every day will be a beach day.

Well, life is grand, but every plant does not grow, and, thank goodness, every day is not a beach day. If you want beach days, don't open a nursery. On gloriously hot summer days when there's nothing better than jumping in the ocean, you'll instead be dragging the hose around trying to save poor little plants from expiring, and trying to talk customers into stepping into some shade to ask that inevitable question about how much sun this plant needs: "If you're in Florida, probably not as much as it's gonna get."

In the dog days of Florida summer, my staff has threatened for years to put a sign on the front door saying, "PLEASE COME IN. We're not coming out."

And don't think parts of Florida don't get cold. I may be tarred-and-feathered by the Chamber of Commerce for admitting it, but sometimes it actually freezes here. Like every winter. And, following a week or two of 80-degree temps, a freeze in Florida can fall like an avalanche. Plants don't take kindly to that.

And on top of that, there's no soil here—I mean NO soil. In some areas, the sand goes down as far as you can dig (if, that is, you don't garden atop a coral outcropping). Water your garden, and 20 minutes later it will be as dry as the proverbial bone. Add compost seasonally—really!—because by the next season you won't be able to tell that any organic matter ever existed there. And in Florida, if it doesn't die of drought, a poor plant might well die of too much water from the ubiquitous sprinkler systems.

Tough plants? My friend Felder Rushing is right: if it's a tried and true survivor in Florida, it's tough.

One of my favorite customers is the one who comes in earnestly asking for what she can plant in a pot by her front door in full sun that won't need water because she's not going to be at the beach house very often to water it. Oh, and by the way, it needs to bloom all the time . . .

We take her around the back of the greenhouse to show her the plastic Easter lilies.

Randy Harelson
The Gourd Garden and Curiosity Shop
Seagrove Beach, Florida

Green
SIDE UP

This book is about nearly indestructible plants. Its aim is to increase the satisfaction of people who garden—without a lot of "bells and whistles" science—by presenting what decades of experience have shown to be the toughest survivors in Florida gardens.

Here you will find the kinds of plants that the state's top garden experts agree are beautiful, adaptable, useful, and downright easy to grow. They just keep on going, even when planted in miserable sandy soils, and survive back-to-back floods, droughts, sudden frosts, torrid summer heat, hurricanes, and benign neglect. A few of the plants are common as sand, even considered "weedy" in some gardens; others are cutting-edge new varieties. All can be used very successfully in any garden style, from suburban front yards to the finest botanical gardens.

You won't find a lot of horticultural instruction in this book, for two reasons: It is covered thoroughly in nearly every other Florida garden book, some of which you probably already have, and most of these plants simply don't need a lot of attention. Most require only two acts on your part: Dig a hole, and plant them "green side up." Water occasionally if it doesn't rain.

You don't have to know a plant's scientific or Latin name to grow and enjoy it. In this book the plants are listed by the most commonly accepted common names, but I include the scientific ones if you want to find out more. A lot of "cultivars" are indicated within single quotation marks. What is important is that you give the plants a try and, if you like them, make an effort to know their names in case you want to tell other folks about them.

Stuck in the Middle with You

In spite of the regional bickering between horticulturists (which reminds me of the old Stealer's Wheels hit song, "Clowns to the left of me, jokers to the right, here I am—stuck in the middle with you"), I find that Florida gardeners are basically like those in other states. Sure, plants change dramatically from one end of the state to the other, even from those on either coast to the ones in the higher middle ground that runs from Orlando straight north to the

Georgia state line. And there really are two Floridas—newcomers in tightly-scripted, gated communities may not have a lot in common with those in small towns and mobile home parks.

But some universal truths have been uncovered about gardening in the Sunshine State. For example, gardeners are about the same in their enthusiasm. The challenges of climate and soils affect us all, and we go about finding solutions with the same gusto. High-end tropical plant collectors in West Palm Beach have nothing over backyard daylily hybridizers in Niceville. Miserable native soil and palmetto bugs the size of brown shoes affect us all equally. Looming state-wide water shortages, onslaughts of invasive exotic plants, and a crushing influx of new gardeners are major ecological issues. The more direct concerns are every gardener's frustration over getting water to cherished garden plants on a weekly basis, weeding the flower bed, and getting along with new neighbors from who-knows-where. This book attempts to deal with all types of gardeners equally.

Scratching and Sniffing

From my very first horticultural tour of tropical plants in the Keys back in the mid 1970's, I have worked with university horticulturists, botanical garden

THE LATE GARDEN AUTHOR HENRY MITCHELL wrote that "there are only two kinds of people—those who garden, and those who do not." Truth is, most of us are basically lawn mowers and shrub pruners, with maybe a potted plant or two on the patio to look at through the window while we are glued to the Weather Channel inside.

Yet most of us remember grandmothers and aunts, even dads and uncles, who grew all sorts of interesting stuff. Truth is, we need to grow something—anything—that depends on us at least a little bit, or as my friend Russell Studebaker, world famous horticulturist from Tulsa, Oklahoma, says, "We'd just as well be sittin' around polishin' our silverware."

staffs, and Disney educators, helped in-laws with landscape problems in Orlando, camped with my wife and friends on barrier islands in the Gulf, seen bikini-clad co-eds sunbathing near alligators in Gainesville, and lectured from Pensacola and Panama City to Tallahassee, Daytona, Jacksonville, Tampa, Gainesville, Ft. Lauderdale, Miami, and West Palm Beach. I have toured both high-tech Cape Canaveral and the amazingly low-tech Coral Castle.

But I have also explored hundreds of miles of Florida's back roads and highways, crisscrossing the state in every season, from Apalachicola to Zephyrhills and beyond, in search of the mainstay "comfort" plants in the wonderfully honest, garden-variety gardens of rural areas and small towns, back alleys, even dozens of mobile home parks. I have driven the entire coastline—all 1,300-plus miles, both coasts, twice—"scratching and sniffing" for great plant combinations growing in as near zero maintenance as can be done.

Observations and Opinions

Through it all, it is my observation that, sadly, many people seem to have gotten away from gardening. Blame it on TV or fast food or global warming, or preening dilettantes who make us feel bad if we don't garden exactly the way they recommend. Better yet, forget the excuses—there are at least eight very simple and understandable reasons why good people, even flower lovers, often have miserable gardens:

- Too tied up mentally, physically, and emotionally with our lives—family, church, meetings, sports, housework, the Internet, cleaning up after hurricanes, and myriad other distractions that preoccupy us. There isn't enough time to garden just for the love of it, so a lot of it becomes a chore.

- The weather won't cooperate when the mood for gardening strikes us; it's either too hot, wet, or dry, too dark after work, or just plain too much humidity to overcome. And the Weather Channel says more is on the way.
- Our bodies ache just thinking about the physical challenges of gardening. After even half a day of planting in the shifting sand, our backs and knees tell us to head for the easy chair by the TV.
- Spiders, snakes, lizards, and bees unnerve us, and we are worried about whatever mosquitoes might be carrying this year. It's less scary to just stay inside and stare through the plate glass window.
- Too many rules to remember for how to garden, what to do, and when. We feel daunted, as if we will mess up or waste time and money no matter what.
- The neighbors talk about us if we garden publicly. We don't want to look like fanatics, so we plant in the backyard and just mow the front.
- Bugs and blights ruin our best efforts, making our gardens look bad and perform poorly. And though there seem to be way too many pests in Florida, we realize that pesticides are bad for the environment and our health. Even "natural" kinds of pesticides are expensive and a lot of fuss.
- Plants die anyway, no matter what we do or how hard we try. So we give up.

There is a simple solution to all the above: Find and plant things that grow themselves whether we tend to them or not! And arrange them in combinations that make neighbors at least think we know what we are doing.

THE FLORIDA PLANT OF THE YEAR program, sponsored by the Florida Nursery, Grower, and Landscape Association, was begun in 1998 to promote the use of superior and proven Florida plants. Benefiting growers, garden centers, and consumers alike, the plants are nominated by the industry and are evaluated by growers, horticulturists, retailers, landscape professionals, and University of Florida faculty.

Those that have been selected as Florida Plant of the Year are noted as such in this book, in their descriptions. You could have an entire landscape using only these plants, and it would be beautiful, and low maintenance, too.

Criteria Used for Selecting the Plants for This Book

Of the thousands of plants we can possibly grow, including old favorites and exciting new cultivars, many disappear because they simply aren't tough enough. The plants in this book, which are the compilation of years of observation by ten of Florida's top garden gurus, have been selected because they have these qualities:

- Are grown in all or most parts of Florida.
- Possess strong values, such as beauty, better flavor or fragrance, multiple-season interest, or are heirlooms.
- Grow in ordinary soil or sand with minimum or no watering or fertilizing.
- Tolerate local climate and weather extremes.
- Resist insect pests and diseases.
- Don't require gardeners to have horticulture degrees—they all but grow themselves.
- Are "no fuss" and easy to groom in the off-season.
- Most can be found at local garden centers or through mail-order sources.

MASTER GARDENERS are men and women who have been given many hours of intense training in all aspects of home horticulture by University of Florida Extension Service professionals. In return, they give an equal number of hours (sometimes many, many more) teaching others about gardening. They are the "take it to the streets" arm of the university.

Take it from someone who has worked with university horticulturists in over forty states, Florida's Extension horticulture agents are top-notch, with a higher-than-average enthusiasm and commitment to doing what is right by you, your garden, and the environment. Swing by your county office to meet the agents and their Master Gardeners, and pick up free, often locally written publications and fact sheets.

No Hardiness Maps

The USDA Hardiness Zone Map is not included in this book, for one simple reason: It is based on "average low temperatures," which are often way off base in Florida. The American Horticultural Society's Heat Zone Map is based on average high temperatures and is another good indicator, but not entirely useful by itself. What we need is to overlay both maps, plus a humidity map, and a wet-winter map, a hot-humid-dry-summer map, a clay-sand-alkaline-acidic soil map, and a "too tired and hot to garden" map. Then we'll have something useful!

Meanwhile the plants recommended here have generally been proven good for all of Florida, unless otherwise noted—as one gardener wrote on an Internet site, "What thrives in the Panhandle may fry in the Keys," and vice versa. In general, Gainesville is at the bottom of North Florida, Orlando and Tampa are in Central Florida, and from there down is South Florida. Any more detail than that can get tedious, except to hardcore horticulturists—and this book is not for them anyway!

"Best for Beginners" and "Kinda Tricky" Lists

No two gardeners will ever agree on a list of "best" and "worst" plants, because of personal experiences and bias. For example, goldenrod—one of our most common roadside beauties—is generally considered "weedy" in America, yet is one of the most popular summer and fall cut-flower perennials in European gardens. One gardener can grow tomatoes with no trouble at all, while neighbors struggle with the challenge. My grandmother grew blue-ribbon African violets, but they quickly melt under my hit-or-miss care.

Some plants are so easy to grow that they are considered too common. Instead of holding our noses in the air, we should celebrate them as great "intro" plants for new or beginner gardeners, especially children who have no expectations, and new home gardeners. The "Best for Beginners" lists scattered throughout the book are good starter plants, which often remain popular long after their success has started to wear thin with more advanced gardeners.

On the other hand, after a quarter-century of watching all sorts of gardeners, and helping them with problems, I have seen too many popular plants succumb to insect or mite pests, foliage and root diseases, and poor adaptation to their climate, or they require frequent maintenance such as pruning or deadheading. These plants—though very popular, and widely sold in garden centers—tend to cause headaches for beginning gardeners, or gardeners who don't get around to preventive maintenance. These are on my "Kinda Tricky" lists. You can grow them all, from both lists, but don't say I didn't warn you about some of them! And just remember, one gardener's weed is another gardener's wildflower.

The Five-Dollar Hole

I was taught in college that it is better to put a fifty-cent plant in a five-dollar hole, than a five-dollar plant in a fifty-cent hole. This means adding organic matter to your soil when planting new stuff, which is often crucial to early plant survival.

Florida soils are very different from the soil in most other parts of the country. Its sand content allows water and nutrients to slip right through, and the high temperatures and rainfall cause organic matter to quickly decompose and disappear.

Yet adding too much organic matter can cause soils to hold too much water during wet seasons, dry out quickly in hot summers, and keep roots confined to a small area. Some landscapers add little or none, preferring to use plants that grow well in native soils or sand; however, in most gardens, a moderate approach usually works best. Think "crackers in chili"—dig your soil a shovel's depth, turning it upside down and chopping up any clumps. Spread

over the area a layer of organic
material (compost, manure, potting
soil, finely ground bark, whatever),
and stir it into the native soil.

A rule of thumb for how much
organic matter to add: trees, tough
shrubs, and bulbs, add little or
none; roses and perennials, add a
one- to two-inch layer of new
material over the native soil, and
stir it in; annuals, add a two- to
three-inch layer. I never add more
than this, and I don't think you
should, either! **Special Note:** Many
tough plants die from being pulled
out of pots and plugged right into
the ground "as is"—their potting
soil keeps roots in a wet-dry cycle
that leads to rot. Always loosen
potting soil from around store-
bought plant roots—trees, shrubs,
perennials, even annuals—and mix
it into your soil.

Mulches Make a Difference

Blanketing the soil with a "skin" of porous material has several benefits: It
keeps the soil surface from packing and crusting in heavy rains, shades and
cools the soil in the summer (like a hat on a bare head), reduces rapid temperature changes during sunny winter days and cool nights, prevents many
weed seeds from getting the sun they need to sprout, and keeps things
looking neat. Landscape fabrics do a fair job, but natural mulches of leaves,
pine straw, compost, or shredded bark "feed" the soil as they compost or are
eaten and taken deep around roots by earthworms. My rule of thumb for
how much mulch to use: Spread your preferred material over the area
deep enough to completely cover the soil, then add that much more to

compensate for settling and natural composting. Refresh once or twice a year as needed.

Two Rules for Composting

Too much has been written and said about composting. It makes me tired just thinking about all I'm supposed to do: small particle sizes, correct carbon-nitrogen ratio, thermophilic bacteria, bins an exact size, turning and aerating, and all the rest of that stuff! As anyone with a leaf pile will attest, there are only two rules for composting: Stop throwing that stuff away, and pile it up somewhere. The rest is finesse. If you are in a compost race with someone, call your county Extension Service office for a handout on how to speed things up. Otherwise, forget the rules—just do it!

Water Wisely

There is no good advice for watering tough plants—after all, many have survived on rainfall alone, as a drive past older gardens in small towns and along country roads can attest. "Drought tolerant" means a plant can go weeks without supplemental water. Potted plants, summer annuals, and a nicely maintained lawn need watering fairly often, but well-established trees and shrubs barely need any water at all; watering woody plants and perennials too often keeps roots shallow and needy.

Below are a few tried-and-true water saving tips:

- Landscape with drought tolerant plants.
- Group plants together based on their water needs.
- Mulch to retain moisture and reduce weeds, and feed the soil.
- Use mulches and groundcovers instead of large expanses of lawn.
- Water at the base of plants, not overhead, to reduce evaporation.
- Water deeply, not frequently; soaker hoses and drip irrigation are more efficient and less troublesome for disease-prone plants than overhead watering. **HINT:** Water twice, giving the first watering time to soak in; the second watering really pushes it down deep.
- Place a shut-off valve on the end of your hose to control the flow and use only what you need.
- Raise your lawn mower height a notch or two, and feed the lawn only lightly with slow-release fertilizer.

- Water lawns no more than once or twice a week in the summer, once every two or three weeks in the winter.
- Place used cans around your yard to collect and measure the water applied in half an hour of irrigating. One-half to three-fourths of an inch is about all a lawn can use at one time. Really.

Remember that water does not necessarily equal love—too much may not be a good thing.

Feed Plants for Quality, Not Quantity

Many tough plants can go for years without fertilizers—just look around and see for yourself. But an occasional feeding can boost their performance and invigorate them with healthier leaves, stems, roots, and flowers.

Though specialty plant fertilizers (palm food, rose food, etc.) are perfectly fine, it is acceptable to just use an all-purpose, numbers-all-the-same plant food (like 10:10:10 or similar) once or twice a year; country folks have done

Soil pH—Not a Big Deal?

I hate to debunk a big myth, but the importance of soil pH—the 1-to-14 scale indicating whether a soil is acidic or alkaline, which influences the chemical form of nutrients in the soil and microbial processes—is often exaggerated. While farmers, horticulturists, and some plant hobbyists need to pay close attention to all aspects of their soils, most gardeners really don't.

Besides, what we do—adding lime to acid soils, or sulfur to alkaline soils—rarely changes things appreciably, or for long. In the garden, ups and downs are worse for plants than whatever pH is naturally present; for most gardens, the best solution is to simply work lots of organic matter into flower beds, and avoid the handful of plants that really do care about pH.

- Prefer acidic soils (below 6): azalea, blueberry, blue hydrangea, ixora, camellia, American holly
- Prefer alkaline soils (above 7.5): butterfly bush, pink hydrangea, red cedar, yucca
- Don't really care about pH: ivy, lantana, banana, crape myrtle, palms, oleander, pines, croton, pyracantha, turfgrasses, and nearly every other tough landscape plant

this for decades. For foliage plants, it's okay to use a fertilizer with a higher first number (nitrogen); for flowering or fruiting plants, use one with a higher middle number (phosphorous. **Note:** Many Florida soils are naturally high in this.). Use liquid fertilizers frequently, as they wash away quickly.

I use just two kinds of fertilizers—a balanced, all-purpose fertilizer once or twice a year, and compost to feed the soil with slow-acting natural ingredients. That's it, and it works. The main thing is, just don't ever overdo it—lean and mean is the best way to keep plants growing but still tough.

Pests and Critters

Florida, whose state bird I think should be the palmetto bug, is full of *creepy crawlies*. Roaches, spiders (including black widows), scorpions, centipedes, snakes, snails, fire ants, nematodes, mole crickets, voles, deer, and mutant grasshopper "lubbers" are all just part of life, and some of them make their way indoors from time to time. Some we simply don't understand, or they are *more nuisances than pests*. Controls are available for a few critters, but for others there is nothing practical. Contact your county Extension Service for good advice before spending a lot of money out of fear or frustration. As one University of Florida scientist put it, "Bugs are not going to inherit the earth—they already own it. Get used to them."

Take off your glasses, and a lot of garden headaches disappear. If you have to, try natural pesticides, or just soapy water. But if a plant continues to suffer, it may be best to simply dump it for another plant—it ain't like y'all are married!

Landscaping with Tough Plants

Believe me, as a garden writer of over a dozen books, I can "wax eloquent" on most aspects of landscaping and gardening. But the truth is, there isn't a whole lot that you *have to do* to be a reasonably successful gardener. The two most important factors are choosing good plants (the topic of this book), and planting them *fairly well.* After that, watering wisely, occasional fertilizing, and a little trimming are the most routine things good gardeners really need to do. Unlike gardening, landscaping is much more than just sticking plants in the ground. Study your space, look around, and at least consider different styles and combinations. Choose plants wisely, get them really well established (with plenty of water the first summer), then go with the flow.

Here are a few tricks for getting more use, with less effort, out of your garden:

- **LOOK AT YOUR GARDEN.** Is it visible from inside the house or from the porch or deck, or do you have to walk out to the street and turn around to see it? Plant stuff you can see from your own point of view—focal points, plant groupings, whatever. You should only have to do so much to please neighbors; as the saying goes, no matter what you do or how you do it, your neighbors are going to talk about you anyway!
- **LESSEN YOUR WORST CHORE.** Mowing, watering, weeding, whatever, find a solution. Make your lawn smaller with fewer edges and corners, create more mulched areas, care for fewer potted plants, etc.
- **MAKE WAVES—OR AT LEAST CURVES.** We are boxed in with lines all around us; why emphasize them in the garden? Good feng shui says lose the angles and the "poison arrow" straight lines, using more curves and hidden delights.
- **STOP STARING INTO THIN AIR,** and put something out there to look at—a bird feeder, pretty plants, garden sculpture (have fun!), water feature, smiley face on the fence, even a mirror—whatever. Just don't stare at your neighbors staring back at you.
- **SIT IN YOUR GARDEN.** No place to sit? Make a place! And make it comfortable, whatever it takes. Then sit there long enough to relax, and see what you see. And do something to make it smell and sound nice, too.
- **FLAT IS BORING.** Add a berm or a treehouse.
- **ADD THESE:** Water feature, "hard feature" accents to catch the eye and draw you into the composition, evening lighting and fragrant plants, outdoor dining area, music.

Advice to Florida Gardening Newbies

You're not in Kansas anymore—but it ain't all Margaritaville either! Forget what you used to know, it's a whole new thing.

First and foremost, resist the urge to grow Northern plants here. They don't, at least not well. Forget about hostas, Japanese maples, and peonies. It may be borderline possible to get them to live, but quality of life is a big issue in Florida—and there is a special room in gardening purgatory for people who torture plants, even for nostalgia's sake.

My sister-in-law from Cleveland, Ohio, who moved to Orlando from southern California, hints broadly to everyone around her about how much she hates the weather, bugs, flatness, pretty much everything. "It's not what everyone likes," she insists, from the relative comfort of her screened-in swimming pool. Do you, also, miss autumn colors, lilacs, and fresh rhubarb pie? Want to create a Northern or Midwestern garden? Try these tricks:

- Get rid of all palms and elephant's ears, and plant arborvitae and junipers instead.
- Edge your lawn so tightly it cuts you just to look at it, but sow a few crabgrass seeds.
- Put out a matching pair of half whiskey barrels with fake geraniums, then spread paper or silk leaves from the craft shop on the lawn.
- Then go inside, call someone from "back home" and whine about the humidity. Listen to the silence on the other end of the line. That should cure you.

Seriously, get rid of the books you used to have, and read the local garden columnist. Meet your county Extension agents and Master Gardeners, and pick up their free publications. Take notes as you visit botanical gardens and explore nearby neighborhoods to see how the usual palette of plants grows.

Try to have fun and experiment—celebrate your failures, because you will learn more from them than from your successes. You will soon prove to yourself—if not to your Northern naysayers (even yourself)—that gardening in Florida isn't all that tough!

Annuals
THAT ENDURE

It's a given, in the gardening world, that a lot of popular plants live for only a short time and then die no matter what you do. Some are true annuals (grow, flower, set seed, then die in one season), some are tender perennials that just don't love our climate, and others are tropical plants that are cheap or easy to plant outside just for the growing season, rather than keeping them indoors part of the year. Regardless of how long these plants can potentially live they are all treated as annuals.

Every seed catalog and garden book has lots of information on growing annuals, but the best knowledge comes from experience. The plants in this book have been grown for many years with little or no effort throughout Florida and are presented here in a "best of the best" list to help you get started with as little effort as possible. Some reseed themselves to "come back" many years on their own; others have seeds that are easily saved from year to year or are readily available at garden centers or through mail order. A few are hard to grow from seed, but cuttings are easily rooted or they can be purchased as rooted plants.

In all but the very southernmost tip of Florida, there are two seasons for these annual plants: the "warm season" (the months of March to November, with long days and warm, muggy nights) and the "cool season" (the months of November through February, which have short days and cool or even frosty nights). In the long, long spring-to-fall part of the year, even some "warm season" plants can burn out

Coleus

Cosmos

from exhaustion, and need replacing, or at least cutting back and fertilizing, to get them through the long haul.

Soil preparation involves digging your soil at least a shovel's depth, usually with a shovel or small power cultivator, then working in lots of organic matter such as compost, soil conditioner, peat moss, composted manure, or potting soil. This helps roots grow quickly and deeply, and helps hold moisture and nutrients. Generally, a layer of organic matter two or three inches deep (certainly no more than four inches deep), spread over the prepared area and then tilled in, will work wonders throughout most of the season. It is better to use a little of each of two or three different kinds of organic matter, than a lot of just one kind.

Fertilize by adding a small amount of a balanced or all-purpose fertilizer to your soil during soil preparation or at planting time, and again every month or two (or three) to replace what is washed away. Most gardeners would agree that using a slow-acting, "timed-release" fertilizer is better for your plants than a hit-or-miss liquid feeding every few weeks.

Mulching simply means covering the newly worked soil with a layer of pine straw, or shredded or chipped bark, to keep the sun from overheating the soil, to keep the soil from crusting over after hard rains or watering, and to slow the germination of weed seeds. This is very important for annual plantings in Florida!

Watering is necessary for most annuals in Florida, especially when it is hot and dry in the summer or during long spells of sunny, windy weather in the

ANNUALS ARE USED FOR FAST COLOR OR SCREENING, as container plants and hanging baskets, for vegetables or herbs, and in long-blooming masses or specimen plants. They provide all-season "color bridges" as perennials flush in and out of show, can give solid color in the winter or summer (even in the shade), and add interest to shrubbery when it is out of season.

winter. How often to water and how much to use is variable; the rule of thumb is to water only when needed, but do it twice—once to "set up" the soil and the second one, done a few minutes after the first, to really soak in and last longer.

Weed control—sorry about this, but it's true—is usually done by hand pulling, chopping with a sharp hoe, mulching to keep seeds from sprouting, or, in last-case scenarios, using chemical weed killers, which are not always dependable or safe for other plants. For information on weed control, consult your county Extension Service agent or ask a dependable, trained garden center employee to show you products that have your kinds of weeds and your kinds of plants listed on the labels. When in doubt, just put on gloves and pull!

Most of these plants have few pests, and practically none that are major. Occasional leaf spots and minor insect or mite infestations can make some plants look bad, but it is still a good idea to avoid pesticides whenever possible in order to protect bees, butterflies, and other beneficial creatures. When possible, choose a "natural" product such as insecticidal soap or neem oil, and be prepared to simply pull up annuals that are suffering intolerable problems—something else is always waiting to go in that hole!

Burgundy Mustard

 Best for Beginners:

- *Celosia*
- *Coleus*
- *Dusty Miller*
- *Globe Amaranth*
- *Moss Rose*
- *Okra*
- *Ornamental Sweet Potato*
- *Pentas*
- *Pansy*
- *Pepper*
- *Periwinkle*
- *Zinnia*

Kinda Tricky:

- *Impatiens* (watering without root rot)
- *Marigold* (spider mites)
- *Sweet Pea* (weird weather)
- *Tomato* (pests, training)
- *Verbena* (mites)

Basil

Ocimum basilicum

Sun or light shade

Basil is one of the simplest and most useful culinary herbs gardeners are likely to grow, especially if you grow tomatoes, which basil complements beautifully. It can be an outstanding butterfly attractor, and some types are perennial in South Florida.

FLOWER: Spikes of small white or pale lavender mint-like flowers from spring to fall.

PLANT: Upright or rounded shrubby plant with highly fragrant foliage of green, dark purple, or green with purplish veins and petioles.

INTERESTING KINDS: Sweet basil is the most popular for cooking, but there are other flavors, including licorice 'Siam Queen' and lemon basil (*O. citriodorum*). 'Spicy Globe' is basketball shaped. There are many purple or burgundy kinds. The best for butterflies is the large 'African Blue'.

Celosia

Celosia argentea var. *cristata*

Sun

These plants will grow in sidewalk cracks and reseed themselves for years to come. Use as a specimen, in combinations, or in masses.

FLOWER: Cockscomb (Cristata group) has rounded, fissured heads up to a foot across of blood red and other colors; plume cockscomb (Plumosa group) has smaller plumes of red, pink, golden, or white; another type (Spicata group) has long, slender flower heads in pink or yellow.

PLANT: Summer annual with pointed oval leaves of medium green or purplish, up to two feet or more tall and half as wide.

INTERESTING KINDS: In the Spicata group, 'Flamingo Feather' is four feet with tall, narrow spikes of pink and white; 'Flamingo Purple' has dark purplish green leaves and pinkish purple spikes; 'Pink Castle' has rose pink spikes. The popular 'New Look' celosia has red leaves.

Cleome or Spider Flower
Cleome hassleriana
Sun or light shade

Tall fluffy plants with marijuana-like, palmate leaves. Good cut flower that wilts when first cut but perks up in water. Excellent butterfly and hummingbird plant, great in masses behind other flowers or combined with bold textured plants in large containers.

FLOWER: Airy heads twelve inches wide and loosely arranged, with open flowers that have spidery "cat whisker" stamens and long narrow seedpods, in white, pink, or dusty purple.

PLANT: Four- to six-foot branching summer annual (there are dwarf forms also) with palm-like foliage that is sticky and has a not-so-nice aroma when cut, and small prickly thorns.

INTERESTING KINDS: 'Helen Campbell' is snow white. There are a number of "Queens" (cherry, pink, rose, purple, mauve, ruby). The Sparkler Series is very compact.

Coleus
Solenostemon scutellarioides
Light shade or sun

Coleus is an old-fashioned tropical foliage plant grown mostly in light shade as a summer annual, either in beds or containers. Large masses are spectacular all summer and fall, and when in flower are fair butterfly plants. Very easy to root in water or moist potting soil and keep indoors over the winter.

FLOWER: Tall flower spikes are studded with small, salvia-like blue trumpets. Most gardeners pinch the stalks off to promote new leaf production.

PLANT: Shrubby, many-branched member of the mint family with large leaves, up to six or more inches long and nearly as wide, in many colors, including red, green, yellow, chartreuse, orange, salmon, pink, and purple, most variegated, splotched, or with contrasting edges. Needs regular water and feeding. Leaves can be steeped to make a tea-like tonic.

INTERESTING KINDS: Seed-grown coleus come in a wide array of leaf shapes and colors. "Sun" coleus, many with burgundy or red foliage, can tolerate hot sun; in University of Florida trials, 'Dark Star' and 'Lime Light' outlived all others when the water was discontinued. Others include 'Plum Parfait', 'Burgundy Sun', and the Florida City Series.

Coreopsis or Tickseed
Coreopsis species
Sun

These common prairie wildflowers "tame" very well in urban flower borders, containers, and butterfly or cut-flower gardens. It is the state wildflower of Florida. Many species are perennial, though some are short-lived.

FLOWER: Cheerful yellow disks two or more inches across from mid-spring through midsummer.

PLANT: Short, stocky clump of linear foliage appears in early winter. Some species have wide, strap-like leaves; others have very delicate, needle-like foliage.

INTERESTING KINDS: *Coreopsis tinctoria* is an airy, openly branched plant, which has a reddish aura around the flower center and finely divided, almost ferny leaves.

Cosmos
Cosmos sulphureus
Sun

This summer and fall flowering showstopper is one of the most impressive flowers of the season and reseeds itself to the point of being a nuisance. But it's easy to thin out seedlings in the spring and summer.

FLOWER: Showy, single, flat, daisy-like flowers in deep orange-yellow.

PLANT: Large branching plant to eight feet with deep-green, divided, marigold-like leaves.

INTERESTING KINDS: Common cosmos (*Cosmos bipinnatus*) has pink, white, rose, or crimson flowers with yellow centers that bloom in the spring, summer, and fall; very easy from seed sown in spring.

Dragonwing Begonia
Begonia hybrids
Sun or partial shade

This fairly new cross between tall, leggy "cane" type (angel wing) begonias and tough wax begonias, has the best traits of both. Stunning as a specimen or large container plant for sun or light shade, though it needs protection from strong winds.

FLOWER: Bright begonia flowers bloom as soon as the plant is set out until you get tired of its non-stop cheerfulness.

PLANT: Self-branching, stemmy plant with upright, fleshy shoots packed with large, bright green, glossy "angel wing" leaves. May need pinching, pruning, or staking when it gets too large or floppy. Does not tolerate high wind, but quickly sprouts new branches from broken joints.

INTERESTING KINDS: 'Dragonwing Pink' and 'Dragonwing Red' are equally stunning.

Dusty Miller
Senecio cineraria
Sun or shade

This is the first "white" companion plant I reach for when looking for contrast in container plantings or when working on a patriotic planting. Good, solid white all year, though it does better in the cool season than the hot summer.

FLOWER: Fairly showy, loose clusters of creamy yellow held above the foliage in summer.

PLANT: Upright, spreading, many-branched shrub-like mound to two feet or taller of soft, grayish white foliage; sometimes needs shearing to thicken up the foliage near its base. Perennial in all of Florida, but typically used as a bedding plant with annuals.

INTERESTING KINDS: 'Cirrus' is a dwarf form; 'Silverdust' is very compact and finely textured. Other silvery or white garden plants in the aster family include *Artemisia* and several *Centaurea* species that are also called dusty miller.

Fanflower

Scaevola aemula

Sun or light shade

Cascading blue flowers are hard to come by, and fanflower fills the bill perfectly, especially for large containers, hanging baskets, and retaining walls.

FLOWER: The name comes from the shape of the flowers, which are one-sided like hand-held fans of blue, violet, or white. Very prolific and long blooming, even in hot summers.

PLANT: Cascading or sprawling masses of fleshy stems covered with small, bright green leaves. Excellent as a groundcover or edging.

INTERESTING KINDS: 'Blue Wonder' and 'New Wonder' are lavender blue; 'Jacob's White' and 'White Charm' are, of course, white. 'Zig Zag' flowers have blue and white stripes.

Globe Amaranth

Gomphrena globosa

Full sun

This historic summer annual, also called bachelor's button, is the perfect companion for other flowers because of its tall, airy growth. Super easy to dry for long lasting flower arrangements. Fair as a butterfly plant.

FLOWER: Bristly, round, button-like clover heads of red, purplish red, pink, or white on long stems up to three feet tall.

PLANT: Often-reseeding summer annual with narrow foliage that is not much to look at. Very pest resistant and incredibly drought and heat tolerant.

INTERESTING KINDS: Compact purplish red 'Buddy', tall red 'Strawberry Fields', and pink 'Lavender Lady'.

Impatiens
Impatiens walleriana
Shade

This very popular shade plant provides a long-lasting splash of color where little else will bloom. It is a cool-season annual in South Florida but a warm-season annual in northern counties, and *must* have shade and lots of water. Great with caladiums.

FLOWER: Showy rounded, red, pink, purple, salmon, white, lavender flowers are produced in great abundance all season long.

PLANT: Round, spreading "bush" with dense, leafy, succulent branches of deep green or variegated foliage. Used in pots, in masses, even as a groundcover in the shade.

INTERESTING KINDS: Many kinds, including Super Elfin and Dazzler Series. New Guinea hybrid impatiens are sturdier and have striking variegated foliage. More sun-tolerant "touch me nots" (*I. balsamina*) are tall, with flowers almost hidden in the foliage.

Jewels of Opar
Talinum paniculatum
Part shade

This very old-fashioned leafy perennial, named after the legendary treasures of the lost continent of Atlantis, is usually grown as an annual, in beds, borders, or containers. Though it reseeds rapidly, it is a very easy plant to thin, leaving just enough to enjoy or share.

FLOWER: Two-foot-tall airy sprays of tiny pink flowers are open only for a day before turning into orange, then golden brown, seed balls.

PLANT: Branching rosette of succulent or fleshy leaves makes a low clump only a foot or so tall and wide. Seedlings are very easy to pull.

INTERESTING KINDS: 'Variegatum' has grayish-green leaves with prominent white margins. 'Kingswood Gold' is nearly chartreuse green.

Johnny Jump-Up

Viola tricolor

Sun or part shade

Favorite "old garden" winter annual, planted in the fall and flowering through the worst winter. Perfect for containers, mass planting, or border edging.

FLOWER: Sweetly fragrant, purple and yellow pansies about the size of a quarter. Blooms fall through spring into summer.

PLANT: Floppy many-branched mounds of small rounded leaves, to a foot or more tall and wide, set out in the fall or winter as transplants. Often reseeds.

INTERESTING KINDS: Various cultivars exist, with flowers ranging from soft lavender to nearly black.

Joseph's Coat

Alternanthera ficoidea

Sun or light shade

Grown entirely for its generally compact form and solid green, golden, burgundy, or variegated foliage, this plant is popular for creating living floral emblems or to spell out words in flower beds. Tolerates close shearing and roots readily (fallen clippings often root in the mulch).

FLOWER: Insignificant white stars throughout the foliage.

PLANT: Solid little "mini-shrubs" from six inches to four or more feet tall.

INTERESTING KINDS: There are many varieties in green, gold, burgundy, rosy red, scarlet, and chartreuse forms. 'Rosea Nana' has rose-colored leaves. 'Golden Threads' has narrow leaves in green, yellow, and white. 'Black Knight' and 'Gail's Choice' are larger deep burgundy shrubs.

Mealycup Sage
Salvia farinacea
Sun

Though this salvia is technically a perennial, it is inexpensive and most often bedded out in masses of small plants as an annual for all-summer spikes of blue or white flowers.

FLOWER: Foot-tall, narrow spikes are densely packed with fairly small flowers continually from spring to frost, which are very attractive to butterflies. Excellent contrast to coarser annuals.

PLANT: Upright, many-branched shrub with narrow leaves that are glossy above, wooly white below. Very fast growing; may break in harsh winds but quickly resprouts

INTERESTING KINDS: 'Victoria Blue' is commonly sold in "six packs" as an annual. 'Victoria White' and 'Cirrus' have white flowers.

Melampodium
Melampodium paludosum
Full sun

Its unfortunate lack of a "common" name scares new gardeners off, but this is one of the top ten summer flowering annuals for massing in hot, dry, parking-lot type garden spots.

FLOWER: Buttery yellow daisies produced in nearly solid sheets, from spring to frost.

PLANT: Mounding plants from two to three feet, with deep green foliage. Requires heat to grow. Reseeds prolifically.

INTERESTING KINDS: 'Showstar' is compact, under two feet tall; 'Medallion' can get over three feet tall and half that wide.

Mexican Sunflower

Tithonia rotundifolia

Full sun

Fast-growing tall screen or accent that flowers nonstop in heat, drought, and humidity, all the while covered with butterflies and hummingbirds.

FLOWER: Marigold-like flowers up to four inches across with yellow or orange petals and yellow centers. Has an extremely long bloom period. Blooms spring to frost. Good as a cut flower and outstanding for butterflies.

PLANT: Large (to six feet or more) multi-branched summer "shrub" with hand-sized leaves. Reseeds well.

INTERESTING KINDS: 'Sundance' and 'Goldfinger' are more compact, to three or four feet.

Mona Lavender Plectranthus

Plectranthus × **'Mona Lavender'**

Shade or part sun

This hybrid relative of "Swedish ivy" and "Cuban oregano" is a fairly new addition to Florida gardens, but has already been named a 2005 Florida Plant of the Year for its splash in shaded gardens and pots.

FLOWER: Six-inch dark purple spikes with inch-long lavender-blue trumpets flecked with darker spots.

PLANT: Small, bushy bedding plant with deep purple stems holding glossy deep green leaves with purple undersides, very striking in masses or pots in light shade.

INTERESTING KINDS: There are other types of plectranthus, but 'Mona Lavender' is outstanding.

33

Moss Rose
Portulaca grandiflora
Full sun

This solid mass of bright flowers opens only for people who are outdoors in the middle of the day. Perfect for rock gardens, edging, and spilling out of containers in hot, dry locations.

FLOWER: Compact, inch-wide, rose-like clusters of brilliant red, magenta, pink, yellow, and white that open only when summer sun shines directly on them, right up until frost.

PLANT: Low mounds, six inches tall by a foot wide, thick with fleshy, cylindrical leaves to an inch long. Reseeds prolifically in hot, dry areas.

INTERESTING KINDS: There are double- and single-flowered strains of cylindrical-leaf moss rose; the popular flowering purslane (*Portulaca umbraticola*) has flat leaves and flat, single flowers.

Nasturtium
Tropaeolum majus
Full sun

Soak the seeds of this cool-season annual overnight, and sow in the fall for flowers all winter and spring. Likes sandy soil (so it's perfect for Florida). Young leaves and large round flowers are perfectly edible.

FLOWER: Round, up to three inches across, in yellow, orange, red, salmon, scarlet or peach.

PLANT: Both bush-type or cascading or sprawling "semi-vine" types are available, with round leaves that are bright green. Too much fertilizer reduces flowering.

INTERESTING KINDS: 'Vesuvius' and the Whirlibird Mix are mounding forms; 'Moonlight' climbs, with pale yellow blossoms; 'Empress of India' has dark scarlet flowers. Out of Africa and Alaska Series have cream-variegated leaves.

Okra

Abelmoschus esculentus

Full sun

Vegetables as ornamentals? You bet! Tall, leafy okra has gorgeous foliage, flowers, and fruit, and makes a statement in large containers or behind other summer flowers. Stems with seedpods make super additions to dried arrangements.

FLOWER: Three-inch, pale yellow, hibiscus-like cups produced near ends of stems.

PLANT: Tall (to six feet), slightly branching stems covered with almost foot-long, deeply divided leaves. Requires hot weather for best growth. Long narrow seedpods are edible when small.

INTERESTING KINDS: 'Burgundy' has reddish green foliage and maroon fruits; 'Blondie' has creamy white fruits.

Pansy and Viola

Viola × *wittrockiana* and
Viola cornuta

Full winter sun or part shade

Pansies and violas have become some of the most popular annuals, and probably the only truly reliable ones for providing color and interest in the cool weather months, connecting fall to the following spring.

FLOWER: Flat and up to four inches across, in white, blue, purple, red, yellow, orange, sometimes with large blotches or contrasting "eyes," produced from fall to late spring. Remove spent flowers for the most optimum continued production.

PLANT: Compact six- to eight-inch-tall mounds of slightly lobed, rounded leaves. Needs cool weather for best growth; generally dies from heat by early summer. Best grown from transplants.

INTERESTING KINDS: There are many hybrid strains and colors of pansies, from big floppy kinds to compact freer-flowering ones. New hybrids, called bedding pansies or violas, between the smaller *Viola cornuta* and the larger pansies have mid-sized flowers and more compact growth, and come in many hues of white, yellow, apricot, blue, purple, and others.

Pentas

Pentas lanceolata

Sun or light shade

This old, tall Victorian "pot plant" has made a huge comeback as one of the best butterfly plants for the summer and fall garden. The shrubby plant, perennial in the southern half of Florida, is mostly used as a bedding and container plant.

FLOWER: Abundant, six-inch-wide clusters of small, starry florets of deep red, white, or pink blooms atop the foliage, giving it its other common name of Egyptian star-cluster. Flowers best in hot weather.

PLANT: Upright, branching shrub, two to five or more feet tall.

INTERESTING KINDS: Many varieties, including 'New Look', but the older, taller strains are best for butterflies.

Pepper

Capsicum annuum

Full sun or light shade

Ornamental peppers, with a huge array of sizes and fruit colors, are seriously overlooked additions to flower beds, herb gardens, and containers. Most ornamental peppers are edible, but very hot!

FLOWER: Small, starry-white flowers from late spring to frost; fruits are tiny birds-eye pods to long and thin, from green to yellow, orange, red, purple, and almost black.

PLANT: Shrubby summer annuals from six inches to four feet or taller, many branched with oval leaves of green, purple, or variegated with white or yellow.

INTERESTING KINDS: There are many, many forms of *Capsicum annuum,* including sweet, jalapeno, and chile peppers. *Capsicum frutescens,* the tabasco pepper, is a large shrub with hundreds of narrow fruits in green, yellow, and red held upright; *C. chinense* includes the habanero pepper which is fiery hot and has beautiful, gnarly orange fruits.

Persian Shield

Strobilanthes dyeranus
Shade or part sun

This plant, perennial in many parts of Florida, is sure to draw comments, whether grown in small groups in the shade, as a single accent, or even as a medium-size filler in a larger pot with white, silver, or burgundy plants.

FLOWER: Short spikes of pale lavender tubular flowers in the winter, not very showy.

PLANT: Leafy shrub to three or four feet tall and nearly as wide. Oval, pointed leaves have a "puckered" texture, and are dark green overlaid with rich purple and tints of shimmery silver. Undersides of leaves are bright purple. Needs water.

INTERESTING KINDS: None yet, but the species is outstanding on its own.

Periwinkle

Catharanthus roseus
Full sun

One of the most drought-tolerant plants on Earth, periwinkle flowers continually with no care at all.

FLOWER: Flat, five-petaled disks of pure white, pink, or red, sometimes with a darker "eye," produced in masses atop foliage from spring to frost, more in hot weather.

PLANT: Compact mound of glossy green foliage up to two feet tall, usually a foot or less. Reseeds prolifically into nearby hot, dry areas. Resents water and heavy wet soils.

INTERESTING KINDS: The Heatwave, Pacifica, and Stardust Series are all popular.

Petunia

Petunia × *hybrida*
Sun

Old reseeding "grandmother's garden" varieties are not as showy, and don't hold up as well in our long, humid summers as modern hybrids, but give a wonderful cottage-garden element to mixed borders and containers.

FLOWER: Flat or ruffled trumpets of white, pink, red, purple, blue, or rose, with or without stripes; some have flowers four inches or more across. Flowers best in cool weather.

PLANT: Sprawling vine-like annual that prefers cool better than extreme heat. May need "pinching" to thicken scraggly growth. Old varieties reseed.

INTERESTING KINDS: Too many to mention, but cascading 'Purple Wave' tolerates heat, needs no pruning, and smells of heavenly spices, all day and night. "Supertunias" and other improved series are extremely popular.

Porterweed

Stachytarpheta jamaicensis
Sun

A surprising native of South Florida, this tall, spreading perennial is usually sold as an annual for butterflies.

FLOWER: Tall, thin, "rat-tail" stems with small purple flowers that open from the bottom of the stem upward for a long flower period. Extremely attractive to butterflies.

PLANT: Mounding plant to over four feet tall and wide with dull green, lightly toothed, pointed-oval leaves up to three or more inches long. May "flop" or split in high winds.

INTERESTING KINDS: Dwarf porterweed generally stays under two feet tall, and can be used as a groundcover. Similar but non-native blue porterweed (*S. urticifolia*) has darker green, quilted leaves. Pink porterweed (*S. mutabilis* 'Coral') has fuzzy light green leaves and very showy pink flowers. There are also porterweeds with red and variegated leaves.

Red Salvia

Salvia coccinea and *Salvia splendens*

Sun or light shade

Salvias are summer mainstays with spikes of red, sometimes pink, purple, white, or peach.

FLOWER: Spikes of small exotic trumpets, mostly red or pink, from spring to frost. Great for butterflies and hummingbirds.

PLANT: Upright, branching, small shrubby plants to two feet tall or more. Solid green leaves give great contrast to the spikes of flowers. Reseeds prolifically everywhere.

INTERESTING KINDS: Native *Salvia coccinea* is the most heat- and drought-tolerant plant of all, is covered with butterflies, and reseeds everywhere. It's the last annual besides periwinkle to die from drought. The most common other summer annual salvia (*S. splendens*) is a mistake to plant in full sun—it does much better in light to moderate shade and needs watering.

Snapdragon

Antirrhinum majus

Sun

One of the best cool-season annuals to plant in the fall or winter, this frost-tolerant plant is fantastic in sunny beds or containers, and continues to be outstanding for winter cut flowers.

FLOWER: Densely-packed spikes of showy red, pink, yellow, lavender, or white thumb-size flowers that can be squeezed on their sides to make them open like snapping dragon mouths.

PLANT: Small upright shrubs, one to two feet tall, with medium green foliage.

INTERESTING KINDS: Many new varieties offer more compact plants, and more open "butterfly-like" flowers, including 'Floral Carpet' and 'Sonnet' selections. Rocket Hybrids are the tallest.

Sweet Potato
Ipomoea batatas
Full sun or moderate shade

Ornamental sweet potatoes, named FNGLA Plant of the Year in 1999, are fast growing, trailing vines with beautiful foliage color for large containers, hanging baskets, or groundcovers. Astounding in masses or entwined with other summer plants.

FLOWER: Not very showy, small "morning glories."

PLANT: Heart-shaped or lobed foliage on long, trailing vines that root as they "run" from spring to frost. Does best in poor soils with low fertility. Forms edible tuberous roots.

INTERESTING KINDS: 'Blackie' has deep burgundy, almost black foliage that is deeply divided; 'Margarita' has shocking chartreuse foliage; 'Pink Frost' ('Tricolor') has variegated white, green, and pink leaves, and is not as vigorous as the other two.

Wax Begonia
Begonia Semperflorens-Cultorum Hybrids
Sun or shade

One of the mainstays of the bedding plant world, this tidy clump of a plant is enjoyed as much for its foliage as its generous flowers in pots, borders, or window boxes.

FLOWER: Cheerful red, white, pink, or salmon flowers with bright yellow stamens are mixed in with and stand above foliage all season long.

PLANT: Rounded mass of slightly scalloped rounded leaves, with a very shiny ("waxy") surface. Foliage can be green, red, or deep bronze. Loved by slugs but replace damage quickly.

INTERESTING KINDS: Many series and "mixes" are available, but those with darker foliage tends to tolerate more sun. The popular Cocktail Series includes 'Vodka', 'Gin', and 'Whiskey'.

Wishbone Flower

Torenia fournieri

Light shade

This spreading mass of foliage and flowers is best described as a "summer pansy" for its non-stop carpet of color. Very tolerant of heat, rain, and light shade.

FLOWER: Tubular white, purple, or deep pink with a yellow spot in each flower's throat, held open with a delicate "wishbone" structure inside, produced in continuous flushes.

PLANT: Low mass of medium green foliage, useful as border edging, mass planting, or cascading from containers, hanging baskets, or window boxes. Reseeds readily.

INTERESTING KINDS: There are several selections in the Summer Wave, Clown, Happy Faces, and Panda Series.

Zinnia

Zinnia species

Sun or very light shade

One of the very best "starter" flowers for kids and adults alike. Outstanding for butterflies and as cut flowers. Best used in masses or behind other plants to hide its ugly lower foliage.

FLOWER: Flat or double daisy-like flower heads, up to three or more inches across, in all possible colors, even white (no black), usually with yellow stamens; produced freely all summer and fall on long stems. Deadheading can increase the number of flowers produced.

PLANT: Many-branching, compact mounds or tall specimens to four feet or more, with pleasing oval leaves. Sometimes prone to powdery mildew but plants keep on flowering. Usually reseeds.

INTERESTING KINDS: Narrow-leaf zinnia (*Zinnia angustifolia* or *Z. linearis*) is a loose mound of smaller, non-stop, orange or white flowers, with outstanding heat and drought tolerance in containers, edging, or rock gardens. The compact Profusion Series is highly resistant to mildew.

Other Fantastic Annuals Worth a Try:

Blue Daze

Ageratum (*Ageratum houstonianum*) is a low growing, spreading edging plant whose cool blue flowers make gardens sparkle in the summer. Some varieties are good cut flowers.

Blue Daze (*Evolvulus glomeratus*) is a spreading, self-branching morning glory relative thick with small, round, gray-green foliage that is very tolerant of reflected heat. Stems root as they grow, forming a dense mat; makes a very good groundcover.

Burgundy Mustard (*Brassica oleracea*, Acephala group) has winter foliage of deep red or maroon, sometimes with white midribs, and tall airy spikes of clear yellow spring flowers. Edible, but hot.

Castor Bean (*Ricinus communis*) is big and bold, perfect for backs of borders or in the center of a bed or large container. These pass-along plants have green or burgundy leaves, but seeds are highly toxic and hard to find commercially.

Cat's Whiskers (*Orthosiphon stamineus*) is a sturdy plant for moist areas with showy white or pale blue flower spikes that are attractive to bees, butterflies, and hummingbirds. A real attention getter.

Cilantro (*Coriandrum sativum*) is a popular seasoning herb used for both its foliage and its seeds (coriander). It grows best over the winter; nick seeds before sowing.

Dill (*Anethum graveolens*) is a sprawling, aromatic herb with fern-like leaves and umbrella-like clusters of yellow flowers that reseeds readily and is a host plant for butterflies.

Flowering Cabbage or **Kale** (*Brassica oleracea* var. *acephala*) is one of the most popular "big" cool season annuals. This bold plant is set out in the fall and provides a striking accent all winter until it sends up tall flower stalks in the spring and fades in the heat.

Gloriosa Daisy or **Black-Eyed Susan** (*Rudbeckia hirta*) and its varieties are very familiar roadside and meadow natives, among the best wildflowers for butterflies and cut flowers.

Heliotrope (*Heliotropium arborescens*) is an old-fashioned favorite that has super-showy, vanilla-scented flower heads in purple, blue, rose, or white all summer. Very salt tolerant, but needs protection from hot afternoon sun. Try 'Fragrant Delight' or 'Blue Wonder'.

Lettuces (*Lactuca sativa*) offer incredible variations of leaf shape and color (mostly greens, golds, and burgundies) for winter and early spring foliage in containers or raised beds. An easy winter edible from seed.

Million Bells (*Calibrachoa* species)—the name says it all with seemingly millions of small, petunia-like flowers on plants that love humidity and well-drained soils. The perfect long-flowering plant for hanging baskets. Can bloom all winter in South Florida. Can tolerate cool weather but not frost in other areas.

Nemesia (*Nemesia* species) is a little-used cool-season or winter annual with masses of very fragrant, cutting-quality flowers on semi-compact plants great for containers, hanging baskets, window boxes, or massed with other plants in beds.

Nicotiana (*Nicotiana alata*) or **flowering tobacco** blooms with panicles of white, red, pink, yellow, or mauve in cool weather; the tall, white flowering tobacco (*N. sylvestris*) is a knockout in the summer shade garden. Some types are highly fragrant.

Parsley (*Petroselinum crispum*), planted in the fall, is an outstanding, frilly mass of bright green foliage all winter, before flowering in the spring. The natural breath freshener is also a major host for butterfly larvae.

Nicotiana

Perilla Magilla (*Perilla frutescens* 'Magilla') looks for all the world like a sun coleus on performance drugs. This brightly colored toughie, with dense stems of plum-red foliage with bright pink and orange leaf markings, holds up in the hottest weather.

Polka Dot Plant (*Hypoestes phyllostachya*) a very old-fashioned plant, sometimes called "freckle face," is a wonderfully understated mass of pink- or white-splashed foliage from spring to fall. Use as a tall summer and fall groundcover or filler between larger plants, in big containers, or around a focal point or statue.

Poppies (*Papaver* species) produce exotic spring flowers from fall-sown seed. Round pods are also attractive; the pods of opium poppy (*P. somniferum*) are the source of opium, which is why this plant is illegal to grow.

Queen Anne's Lace (*Daucus carota*) is the reseeding parent of the carrot, with ferny foliage and large, flat, white heads of flowers. Great for butterflies, in meadows, and in poor soil.

Roselle (*Hibiscus sabdariffa*) is an interesting but invasive old "country" plant, an okra relative whose juicy, burgundy "fruits" (up to sixteen pounds per plant) are made into jelly.

Sweet Alyssum (*Lobularia maritima*) is one of the best cool-season edging or border plants for its spreading, cascading masses of white, pink, or lavender blooms in fall, winter, and spring.

Tomato (*Lycopersicon lycopersicum*) is something every gardener has to try! For easiest success in sandy, nematode-ridden soils, grow bush-type kinds in large containers, and plant at least two crops rather than trying to keep one alive throughout the long, hot summer.

Wild Poinsettia (*Euphorbia heterophylla*) is a "pass-along plant" that those who have it, want to get rid of! The rapidly reseeding little shrubby plant has inch-wide green-and-red poinsettia flower bracts all summer. Interesting, if weedy, and very tough!

Wedding of the Flowers

My great-great-aunt Bernice was a hoot. The retired New Orleans school principal who once took flying lessons from Charles Lindberg, once told me convincingly when I was a kid that flying saucers came from inside the Earth through a hole in Antarctica. When she passed away, I found in her old notebooks a crumbling, printed Victorian parlor word game in which a story was told with blanks left in the narrative, to be filled in with plant names. Here it is, a hundred-year-old "Wedding of the Flowers," with some possible answers underlined:

Black-eyed Susan married Sweet William after he Aster. His rival had been Ragged Robin, but the groom's Tulips sealed the engagement under towering Sunflowers. Their Four O'clock wedding in Virgin Bowers was announced by Bells of Ireland and Bluebells. The bride was given away by Poppy, as the groom's mother whispered to him "Forget-Me-Not". Jack-in-the-Pulpit officiated.

Though the groom was giving up Bachelor Buttons, he brought to his bride Peppermint and Candytuft. The rings, which were held in the Palm of Jon-quil, were made of Goldenrod and the bride's Paper-white gown was trimmed with Queen Anne's Lace (with Cowslips underneath). Bridesmaids included Lily, Daisy, and Rose. Their dresses were Lilac and Pinks, and they received Foxgloves and Cockscombs. The groomsmen were Dan-delion, and Chrys-anthemum.

There was a crowd at the wedding— Phlox—but Seven Sisters and Old Maids were left behind. Singers included Larkspur and the great Bird of Paradise. A brief scene was created when Johnny Jump-up objected to the wedding, but Bleeding Heart, Bittersweet, and Weeping Willow, all rejected lovers of the American Beauty, kept their peace.

They ate their wedding cake from Buttercups, and had Lady Slippers tied behind their carriage. Their new home will be on Cape Jasmine, where they will spend the rest of their Everlasting lives in Sweet Peas (peace), hopefully with Baby's Breath.

Here's hoping their Passionflower love affair, made under the Star of Bethlehem, doesn't turn into Touch-Me-Not!

UNBEATABLE
Bulbs

Flowering bulbs and bulb-like perennials that "come and go" with the seasons are sometimes overlooked by new gardeners, or planted as afterthoughts. But they can easily be worked into overall landscapes to add or prolong color and provide foliage even in "off" seasons.

Not all the plants in this section are true bulbs. Some are rhizomes, corms, tubers, and other forms of underground plant parts used to store energy, water, and food for new growth, and to sustain the plant during dry spells and dormancy.

The planting rule of thumb for true bulbs, unless otherwise indicated, is "twice as deep as they are tall." Big bulbs go deeper than smaller ones (you can even plant smaller ones above larger ones). Most usually require well-drained soil and certainly shouldn't be planted where water stands for hours after a rain. Too much organic matter added around bulbs planted in sandy soils can increase moisture retention and bulbs will rot.

Interplanting with Bulbs

Some bulbs are dormant in the summer; some perennials are completely bare in the winter. Why waste precious garden space for "one shot" plants, when you can plant one with the other to prolong the season? Bonus: The emerging foliage of one can hide the fading leaves of the other. Large shrubs, bare winter lawns, and overstuffed patio pots can all be gussied up with bulbs. The biggest considerations for interplanting flowers include making sure that all of them get the amount of sun or shade they need and that watering or fertilizing one type doesn't harm the others.

Elephant's Ear

Best for Beginners:

- *Amaryllis*
- *Caladium*
- *Canna*
- *Crinum*
- *Elephant's Ear*
- *Ginger*
- *Gladiolus*
- *Lycoris*

Kinda Tricky:

- *Alstroemeria*
- *Caladium*
- *Dahlia*
- *Gloriosa Lily*
- *Kaffir Lily*

Kaffir Lily

Tulips and Daffodils Hate Florida

Tulips are annuals in Florida, period. They are perennials in parts of the world that have cold winters and dry summers, so because of the mild wet winters and hot, humid climate, they usually don't get the "chilling hours" they need to rebloom, or they may rot during long spells of wet, muggy weather. Plus, the new bulbs they produce take energy away from the "mother" bulbs while requiring a couple or more years to get to blooming size, and then everything just peters out. Hyacinths and most daffodils are also best used for one-shot foliage and spring flowers.

Sure, you could dig and clean and store them, and refrigerate them before planting again, but c'mon—what's the point? Buy a cheap sack full every fall, refrigerate them for five or six weeks before planting, then stick them in groups here and there where you want winter texture and spring flowers. Then feed them to the compost.

African Iris

Dietes vegata

Sun or part sun

The "fortnight" lily blooms off and on all spring, summer, and fall, adding splash to shaded borders or in raised beds or rock gardens where it will not rot in rainy weather.

FLOWER: Six-petaled flowers to three inches across consist of three spread-out solid yellow, white, or cream-colored petals in front of three others, with the back three each having a darker spot, all produced on long-lived branched stalks that continue to flower throughout the warm season. Most flowers last only a day, but some hybrids last three.

PLANT: Upright sword-like leaves to three or more feet tall in slow-spreading clumps that rarely need dividing.

INTERESTING KINDS: Hybrid 'Lemon Drops' and 'Orange Drops' have yellow or orange markings.

Amaryllis

Hippeastrum species

Sun, part sun, part shade

Perhaps the easiest "big" bulb to flower—even just sitting on top of the ground or in a pot on a TV—this African native has long been a favorite stalwart of Florida gardens.

FLOWER: Clusters of large, trumpet or bell-shaped flowers in rich red, white, pink, salmon, and red-orange, sometimes with stripes or "picotee" contrasting rims, atop sturdy stems to eighteen inches tall

PLANT: Strap-shaped leaves erupt from a large bulb that usually goes dormant in the late summer and re-emerges in the fall or winter. Can be "forced" to grow indoors in winter. Plant with the bulb neck level with the soil surface.

INTERESTING KINDS: The heirloom Saint Joseph's lily (*H. johnsonii*) is a very tough red with white stripes that flowers well even in shade.

Caladium

Caladium bicolor

Part sun, part shade, shade

There's no better way to bring pizzazz to a shaded border, brighten a dark patio, or skirt a row of gloomy shrubs with color than with inexpensive caladiums. They are outstanding in pots as well. Many will tolerate a lot of sun if watered frequently.

FLOWER: Not very showy whorl of white surrounding a pencil-like pollen stem, mostly hidden in the more desirable foliage. Cut it off to promote more leaves.

PLANT: Mostly pointed heart-, shield- or strap-shaped, up to a foot long, of red, white, pink, and green, in countless combinations. Produced in two-foot-tall masses.

INTERESTING KINDS: There are simply too many to even begin mentioning, quite a few of which were bred in Florida. All are usually sold with photos nearby.

Canna

Canna × generalis

Sun or very light shade

This old Victorian garden mainstay is still one of the most widely planted perennials, grown by both upscale horticulturists and rural gardeners.

FLOWER: Sometimes very showy, gnarly masses of irregularly shaped flowers in orange, red, yellow, apricot, salmon, and mixed. Hard, round, bristly seedpods can be interesting as well, especially on old Indian shot canna (*Canna indica*).

PLANT: Upright masses of slick tropical leaves in green, bronze, dark burgundy, and striped. Very good for container culture, near pools or water gardens, around patios, and in Victorian mixed plantings. Control leaf-roller worms with biological worm sprays.

INTERESTING KINDS: 'Bengal Tiger' has bright yellow stripes with maroon margins and orange flowers; 'Tropicana' has shocking stripes of red, pink, and orange.

Crinum

Crinum species

Sun

No Florida garden should be without this big, coarse bulb! It is often found thriving in cemeteries—I even photographed one growing in broken glass between the sidewalk and curb beside a beer joint.

FLOWER: Stalks up to four feet tall topped with nodding clusters of slender trumpets up to a foot long, either white, pink, wine-red, or white with reddish stripes.

PLANT: Floppy eruptions of long, wide, strap-like leaves remain in large clumps for many years. Dies down in cold weather further north. Tips of new growth sometimes get caught in the twisted dried remains of the previous year's foliage.

INTERESTING KINDS: Nearly red 'Ellen Bosanquet', pink ruffled 'Emma Jones', pink with white streaks 'Carnival', light pink 'Powelii'. Others have burgundy foliage.

Dahlia

Dahlia hybrids

Sun, or part sun

Native to Mexico and Guatemala, this summer-loving plant has spectacular blooms, from the small bedding types set out in borders as annuals, to the large cut-flower dinner-plate-size kinds.

FLOWER: Many-petaled daisy-like flowers from two to twelve inches across. Can be single, double, balls, pompoms, and other shapes, in every color but true blue. Large flowering kinds are excellent cut flowers.

PLANT: Summer-growing, with both short compact varieties and tall kinds that require staking, with leaves divided into many large, deep green or burgundy leaflets. Requires well-drained soil, so plant in raised beds or large containers. Tall kinds may rot in wet weather.

INTERESTING KINDS: Multi-stemmed tree dahlia (*D. imperialis*) can grow well over ten feet tall with daisy-like flowers up to eight inches across.

Elephant's Ear
Alocasia, Colocasia, and *Xanthosoma*
Shade or sun

Elephant's ears typify the tropics. Big, bold, coarse foliage perfectly complements plants both in-ground or in large pots.

FLOWER: Rarely seen calla-like spathe, hidden in the foliage canopy.

PLANT: *Alocasia* is the clump-forming "upright" elephant's ear, with tips pointing upwards. The wetland-invasive *Colocasia,* also called taro or dasheen, has tips pointing downward, on stalks up to four or more feet tall, forming a mass of tropical boldness. Lush, large leaves may need protection from strong winds, which can tear them.

INTERESTING KINDS: There are dark colored and white-variegated forms of both species. 'Hilo Beauty' is a smaller plant with cream mottling and 'Black Magic' is wine colored. *Alocasia* 'Variegata' has cream blotches and 'Violacea' is tinged purple. *Colocasia* 'Fontanesii' and 'Illustris' have dark markings.

Four-O'-Clocks
Mirabilis jalapa
Sun, part sun, part shade

Thomas Jefferson's "marvel of Peru" is perhaps the most fragrant evening flower, highly attractive to hummingbirds and large night-feeding sphinx moths.

FLOWER: Two-inch trumpets with intense fragrance open in late afternoon and close the following morning, in yellow, fuchsia, red, white, or streaked. Green bracts produce dried pea-size seeds that sprout readily.

PLANT: Shrubby perennial three to six feet or more tall and nearly as wide from a large sweet potato-like tuber, often reseeds prolifically to become weedy.

INTERESTING KINDS: Seedlings are highly variable, but can be thinned to single colors. Every flower of 'Broken Colors' is streaked and flecked with red, white, yellow, orange, and red. 'Golden Sparkles' is yellow tipped with pink. 'Baywatch' is a large plant with pale yellow flowers.

Gingers

Various species

Light shade

The gingers, hardy in all parts of Florida, grow best in light shade with lots of mulch and fair amounts of moisture. They have interesting foliage and are among the most exotic flowers of any perennial grown. Most have edible—though zesty or hot—tubers, and make good cut flowers.

Butterfly Ginger

Protect Bulbs from Critters:

Voles are small, mouse-like rodents that burrow and eat roots and (especially) tender bulbs. I have actually seen them in action, watching plants start to wobble and then disappear into tunnels! Not much will control these destructive pests—they are even hard for cats to catch!

Here are some "tricks of the trade" used by hard-core gardeners and botanical gardens to protect bulbs from being eaten:

- When planting bulbs, surround them with gravel or other coarse material, which voles hate to dig through.
- Place "live" traps near burrows, baited with something smeared with peanut butter.
- When digging beds, place hardware cloth (wire mesh with half-inch openings) in the bottom and up the sides, like an upside-down fence. Cut a trench around the beds and line it with the strip of hardware cloth at least six or eight inches tall, partly sticking out of the ground (mulch will cover the exposed part). Make sure the bottom edge is curved outward, away from the bed, to guide voles and moles away, not under.
- Plant individual bulbs or plants in wire baskets buried partially in the ground.
- Protect from digging squirrels, chipmunks, and cats by laying "chicken wire" over the planted area, which bulbs will grow up through.

Butterfly Ginger (*Hedychium coronarium*) is a wide-leaf bamboo-looking plant topped with extremely fragrant white flowers in summer and fall; golden butterfly ginger (*H. flavum*) has buttery-yellow flowers tipped with red; red ginger lily (*H. coccineum*) has orange-scarlet flowers with red stamens, and 'Flaming Torch' (*H. coccineum aurantiacum*) has large spikes of orange flowers.

Hidden Gingers (*Curcuma* species) have very showy spikes of tight, colorful bracts with small flowers in spring or summer that are usually hidden in the foliage, which is canna-like but distinctly pleated, light green or with red midribs. Outstanding species include queen lily (*C. petiolata*), three feet tall with rosy purple bracts; giant plume (*C. elata*), six feet tall with two-foot flower spikes; Siam tulip (*C. alismatifolia*), a small bedding plant with rosy red flowers; and *C. roscoeana* with orange bracts and yellow flowers.

Spiral Gingers (*Costus* species) have sprawling stems with spirally-arranged leaves, and flowering cones produced at the ends of leafy stems in the late summer with colorful bracts. Malay or crepe ginger (*C. speciosus*) is tall with interesting textured leaf undersides (feel them!) and comes in a beautiful variegated

Hidden Ginger

form. Red tower ginger (*C. barbatus*) has large flower cones with dark-red bracts and yellow flowers, and is good for hummingbirds.

Pinecone or **Shampoo Ginger** (*Zingiber zerumbet*) is a true ginger, but one of the showiest for all of Florida with five- to six-foot leafy shoots towering over very interesting, knobby, pine-cone-like flower structures that come up from the ground to a foot or two tall. The cones start out green with small yellow flowers peeking out before the cones turn red. Cones brim with a silky moisture that has long been used as a hair conditioner. 'Darcyi' has cream-striped leaves.

Shell Ginger (*Alpina zerumbet*), one of the most commonly-grown gingers, has stalks of shiny green spear-shaped leaves that grow outward seven to eight feet tall from tight, slow-to-spread clumps. 'Variegata' is a popular form with prominent yellow bands on the leaves; waxy, shell-like flowers marked with red, purple, or brown and very fragrant, hang in clusters on arching stems.

Gladiolus
Gladiolus species and hybrids
Sun

Gladiolus, the ultimate summer cut flower, is as easy as any plant can be. Just stick a handful of corms into the ground, add stakes to keep the tall plants from falling over, and stand back! Plant a few every month for a continuous show.

FLOWER: Narrow, three- to four-foot spikes of showy flaring flowers that open a few at a time all on the same side of the stem, from the bottom up. Outstanding cut flower in red, yellow, orange, apricot, white, purple, and many combinations.

PLANT: Upright fan of sword-like leaves grows from an inexpensive corm.

INTERESTING KINDS: Hardy gladiolus (*Gladiolus communis* ssp. *byzantinus*) is an old-garden variety with bright magenta flowers, sometimes white.

Gloriosa Lily
Gloriosa species
Sun, or part sun

This is one spectacular climbing bulb! A sure attention-getter on an entry or fence.

FLOWER: Each four-inch summer blossom faces downward, but has six wavy-edged petals that curl back upwards, each an eye-catching brilliant red with yellow bands.

PLANT: Climbing to six feet or more by a tendril on the tip of each five- to seven-inch-long leaf that wraps around any wire, string, lattice, or other support. Grows best in warm, moist summers and cool, dry winters—perfect for Florida's climate. If grown in a pot, withhold water when leaves begin to yellow in the fall.

INTERESTING KINDS: G. *superba* and G. *rothschildiana* are similar except for the amount of color in the flowers; some references list them as the same.

Lily of the Nile
Agapanthus orientalis
Sun, part sun, part shade

The "lily of the Nile" is one of the showiest plants for all parts of Florida, most often used as a border or in accent groups, or even massed as a groundcover.

FLOWER: Large round clusters of many dozens of funnel-shaped blue or white flowers on bare stems from two to four or more feet tall.

PLANT: Fountain-like clumps two or three feet tall and wide of glossy, strap-like leaves, that spread slowly and rarely need dividing.

INTERESTING KINDS: Many hybrids and cultivars range in height and flower color (all blue or white). 'Flore Pleno' has double flowers. A. *africanus* is shorter, both in leaves and flower stalks, than common A. *orientalis*.

Naked Ladies
Lycoris squamigera and Amaryllis belladonna
Winter sun, even under deciduous trees

Two different bulbs, but both look very much alike. Though garden club ladies call them "magic," "resurrection," or "surprise" lilies, both kinds are commonly called "naked ladies" because the long-stemmed pink beauties shoot up out of the ground in midsummer with no foliage at all.

FLOWER: Multiple large pink trumpets atop sturdy two-foot or taller bare stems in mid- to late summer.

PLANT: Loose but attractive clumps of medium green leaves from late fall to spring; can be interesting coarse accents in the winter when other plants are dormant. Must have winter sunshine to form summer flower buds.

INTERESTING KINDS: Belladona lily comes only in pink. *Lycoris purpurea* has purplish flowers; *L. sprengeri* is a shorter species; *L. sanguinea* has reddish-orange flowers.

Rain Lily
Zephyranthes species
Sun or part sun

Summer-flowering bulbs that begin to flower with the rainy season add zest to borders and "meadow" lawns that are cut infrequently, and bring interest to mulched areas.

FLOWER: Open or nearly closed funnel-like flowers in pure white, pink, or golden yellow, up to four inches wide, extend above the grass-like foliage and open during rainy spells in the summer.

PLANT: Nondescript six- to twelve-inch-tall grassy clumps.

INTERESTING KINDS: Common pink rain lily (*Z. rosea*) is very showy. White rain lily (*Z. candida*) has pure white flowers tinged with pink on the inside; *Z. grandiflora* has pink flowers that are flat in midday and close in the evening; *Z. citrina* has fragrant yellow flowers. Atamasco lily (*Z. atamasco*) has pink-striped buds that open into pure white flowers.

Spider Lily or Hurricane Lily
Lycoris radiata
Winter sun

One of the most familiar late-summer bulbs, whose flower stems pop up almost magically overnight, without foliage. Excellent summer flower for shady settings, thriving beneath deciduous trees and shrubs, even among groundcovers.

FLOWER: Airy clusters of red flowers with long, spidery stamens, atop naked stems up to eighteen inches tall.

PLANT: Narrow, strap-like leaves, about the size of liriope, with a paler stripe down the center of each, appear in the fall and persist until spring.

INTERESTING KINDS: 'Alba' has white flowers; *L. aurea* (or *L. africanus*) has yellow flowers. A similar bulb is oxblood lily (*Hippeastrum bifidum*), which looks more like a smallish, naked-stem red amaryllis.

Swamp Spider Lily

Hymenocallis species

Sun or part shade

This showy native bulb, often seen blooming in roadside drainage ditches, is one of the few that tolerates—even prefers—damp or wet soils.

FLOWER: Multiple stalks two to three feet tall are topped with groups of fragrant white flowers each up to three or four inches with long, narrow, spidery petals connected with a membranous white center cup.

PLANT: Clumps of strap-like foliage up to three feet tall and wide tolerate shade and heavy or wet soils.

INTERESTING KINDS: Old favorite 'Tropical Giant' has white flowers to six inches across. 'Sulphur Queen' has six-inch yellow flowers. Peruvian daffodil (*H. narcissiflora*, sometimes sold as *Ismene calathina*) has white, green-striped flowers with green throats. Flowers of *H. latifolia* or *H. keyensis* have three-inch cups and five-inch spidery petals.

Tuberose

Polianthes tuberosa

Sun or part sun

A Mexican native noted for its powerfully sweet, gardenia-like fragrance, this summer- and fall-flowering plant is an old-time garden favorite, dating back to its more useful days before deodorants and room fresheners.

FLOWER: Pure white tubes are loosely arranged in clusters near the tops of three-foot stalks.

PLANT: Bulb-like rhizomes spread fairly well into clumps of grassy foliage; they can be left in the ground for many years but can rot if planted in poorly-drained soils. Suitable for growing in containers that can be allowed to dry out in the winter.

INTERESTING KINDS: 'Mexican Single' is the best cut flower. 'The Pearl' is a popular double-flowering form. 'Marginata' has white-edged leaves. *P. howardii* has red-and-green blooms that attract hummingbirds.

Voodoo Lily
Amorphophallus bulbifer
Part shade or shade

No doubt the most unusual bulb for Florida gardens, this creepy woodland or shade plant is perfectly hardy, and sure to get gasps of attention from visitors.

FLOWER: Fleshy, light burgundy stalk with purple spots to three feet tall. The top half bears a slightly unwrapped hood-like bract surrounding a spike-like protrusion, with a temporary aroma of rotten meat to attract pollinating flies. Blooms in the spring.

PLANT: Fat bulb-like tuber shoots up a single three- to four-foot fleshy stalk topped with a wide, deeply-divided, umbrella-like leaf.

INTERESTING KINDS: Flower stalk and leaf stalk of *A. konjac* get up to six feet tall; *A. paeonifolius* gets even larger with a wide, ruffled purple-and-green leafy spathe spotted with white.

Other Great Garden Bulbs:

There are many other kinds of bulbs to try—some are all-time favorites of mine, but may not be as reliable or readily available. Here are a few worth looking for; you can find much more information on growing them in nearly any all-purpose garden book or mail-order catalog.

Blazing Star or **Gayfeather** (*Liatris* species) is a tall, narrow spike of lavender or white; an excellent native for cut flowers or butterflies but not easy to grow because it needs neglect.

Blood Lily (*Scadoxus multiflorus*), an amaryllis relative native to South Africa, is a super-showy spring bloomer that reminds some people of gaudy red disco balls. Hardy to the mid teens, the attention-getting flowers show off best at the front of borders or in pots as strong accents.

Blazing Star

Calla Lily

Calla Lily (*Zantedeschia aethiopica*) is perfectly hardy outdoors, but requires a good bit of moisture to grow and flower well. Excellent as a cut flower, both the white and quite a few yellows and spotted kinds, and is wonderful in containers.

Camassia (*Camassia* species) is a native meadowland bulb that wows gardeners in Europe. It has sword-like leaves and flower spikes up to three feet tall, topped with a loose arrangement of small, starry, blue flowers. It grows and flowers well in boggy gardens or clay soils, even in shade.

Kaffir Lily (*Clivia miniata*) is a shade-loving, frost-sensitive plant often kept in containers, fairly expensive but easy to propagate and share. Showy flowers are on stems above wide, strap-shaped leaves.

Montbretia (*Crocosmia* species) is a rampant spreading mass of floppy, sword-shaped leaves with arching stems of vivid orange-red flowers that seem to sizzle in the summer. It is hardy throughout the South. Popular crocosmia cultivars include red 'Lucifer' and deep yellow 'Jupiter'.

Painted Arum (*Arum italicum*) is a surprising winter-foliaged and spring-

Montbretia

flowering heirloom, most often found in old established gardens where people have swapped plants. It fills a huge gap left where summer perennials have gone dormant for the winter.

BULB FOODS ARE BEST FOR BULBS. Like all plants, bulbs need a balanced fertilizer containing nitrogen, phosphorous, and potash, in small amounts. Bone meal alone has only phosphorous, just one of the main ingredients needed for overall plant health and growth. Researchers at North Carolina State University worked with Dutch bulb growers to develop Holland Bulb Booster and other perfectly formulated brands of bulb food. They're expensive, but they go a long way.

Do You Speak Garden?

Love that *lingua franca*! Comfortable gardeners often speak plain, and plainly, to one another, slipping into a relaxed dance with country sayings and clichés that cause high school English teachers to shudder.

It's not that we don't know better; though cognizant of the often-confusing rules of our language, sometimes we prefer down-home yakking over high falutin' discourse. Some of our quirky descriptors are more meaningful than being precise.

I've picked up a few fun aphorisms from my English gardening buddy Rita Hall, who "bloody falls on her bum" every time she hears someone say they're "fixin' to do" something—which we always seem to be doing: Fixin' to set out some 'maters. Fixin' to blow the leaves. Fixin' to git on a plane, or on a train.

Rita, who "bungs" (crams) plants into the ground, got her "nappies in a twist" (shorts in a knot) when she heard me tell someone that their green tomatoes would "red up" after being picked. "Red up? What's that mean?" she laughed.

Yet she says anyone who doesn't speak in a local jargon is just putting on airs—and real people can tell; after just a few minutes of hearing someone from England talk, Rita can spot their dialect, and pinpoint what part of England they are from. And on two trips to England, I've heard her revert to a normal English accent within an hour of getting through customs.

Jargon rules! A fellow called my radio program the other day to share how his rose bush—which he had pulled out of a pasture using a tractor so he could get the main root—had "growed up so good" that when it flowered "it was just a bo-kay." We all could tell how proud he was.

If you don't understand our patter—from the French word *patois*—you ain't from around here, are you?

Grasses
WITH GUMPTION

Ornamental grasses bring the Florida landscape to life! Shrub-like and groundcover grasses have been grown in botanical and cottage gardens for many decades. The U.S. Department of Agriculture's "bamboo introduction station" for the Southeast United States, located near Savannah, Georgia, has nearly every imaginable variety of bamboo and other grasses, and there are members of the American Bamboo Society in every state who know and grow the very best kinds for landscapes.

Yet other than the common use of pampas grass and bamboo, only fairly recently have grasses become more widely accepted as very tough "foils" to other landscape plants—and now they are being used even around fast-food restaurants! They come in a wide variety of shapes, colors, variegations, textures, and long-stemmed "flowers" that are long lasting in both fresh and dried cut-flower arrangements. Some grasses grow in tight clumps; others "run" or spread. The plants can be used as specimens, in groups, as ground-covers, in naturalistic masses, and even in containers.

Though some prefer shade, and a few tolerate moist soils (some even grow in water gardens), most grow best in sunny, dry locations. They put out new growth in the spring, flower in the summer and fall, and have no major pests.

Even ornamental grasses need "mowing," at least if you want to keep them neat. Most gardeners leave the foliage alone, but some cut the old growth back in the late winter to help new growth come out clean and fresh; be sure to do this before new growth begins to come up, or it may look ragged all summer. There's no real need to do this, other than for cosmetic purposes—if you don't prune the old growth, new foliage will cover it up by late spring. Once a year, in mid- to late winter, give the old foliage a neat shearing so the new spring growth will come out nice and clean. Don't burn, as tempting as it may be, or risk killing the center of the clump, not to

BAMBOO IS NOT THE THUG THAT MANY PEOPLE THINK IT IS. Most gardeners who have problems with bamboo have a "running" kind, generally species of *Phyllostachys* that include "fishing pole" bamboo, giant timber bamboo, the beautiful black bamboo, and others. These very cold-hardy bamboos have almost woody underground stems that can shoot in any direction and, when cut, can send new plants up at every joint. They can take over entire landscapes—and gardens of neighbors, too! Running bamboos can be contained—at least for a while—with trenches, foot-deep edging, and a little luck. Otherwise, herbicides will have to be brought in.

On the other hand, some very beautiful kinds of bamboos stay in slow-to-spread clumps, most of which are not hardy in portions of the South. These are in the *Bambusa* genus, which includes some that get up to ten or more feet high but take many years to spread even a little. *Bambusa* species are root hardy in all parts of Florida, but may get damaged in the Panhandle by temperatures below the mid-teens.

mention losing your eyebrows! Approach grasses from an angle with sharp shears or a fast-running string trimmer, going around and around like eating an ice cream cone, gradually getting down to the main clump.

Bamboo

Bamboos (*Bambusa multiplex*) are a group of generally tall, clump-forming or slow-to-spread grasses with narrow leaves produced in joints of tall, hollow, woody canes. 'Golden Goddess' is not very thick but tall and bushy, making it a good screening plant.

Cordgrass

Cordgrass (*Spartina bakeri*), is an outstanding native grass for lakeside or wet areas. The three- to five-foot upright clumps have a slight curve to the ends of the leaves, and brown flower heads rise above the foliage in May or June.

Crown Grass

Crown Grass (*Paspalum quadrifarium*), named a Florida Plant of the Year in 2003, is a bunch grass, three to four feet tall and wide, whose leaves are dark green all year, though the broad blades roll up when dry and take on a blue-green appearance. Use as an accent or massed planting.

Dwarf Bamboo (*Pleioblastus pygmaeus* or *Arundinaria pygmaea*) is a groundcover bamboo to three feet tall, very thick and aggressive, even in dense shade. Must be contained by walks or deep metal or plastic edging.

Dwarf Bamboo

Fakahatchee Grass or **Gama Grass** (*Tripsacum dactyloides*) is a Florida native that thrives even in wet conditions or light shade. It gets up to six feet tall and wide. Dwarf fakahatchee (*Tripsacum floridanum*) is only about three and a half feet tall and wide, with a finer texture, and can be pruned into a ball.

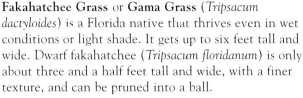

Fakahatchee Grass

Lemon Grass (*Cymbopogon citratus*) is a waist-high grass that produces a strong citrus aroma from its leaves and stems, and is used as a culinary herb or just to make the garden smell a little zesty. It grows well in raised beds and containers, but may freeze in northern counties, so be prepared to bring it indoors for winter.

Lemon Grass

Palm Grass

Palm Grass (*Setaria palmifolia*) looks more like cast-iron plant than a real grass. Its wide leaves are deeply pleated like those of a young palm, but can get eight feet or more tall and wide (less than that in northern counties). 'Variegata' has a white stripe along leaf edges. Palm grass can spread by seed, but makes a good woodland understory plant or foil to thinner-foliaged plants.

Pampas Grass (*Cortaderia selloana*) forms large, rounded, billowy clumps to eight feet or more tall and nearly as wide, with many taller stems of dense, two- to three-foot flower plumes of white or pink in the late summer. Compact form 'Pumila' gets only four to five feet tall.

Pampas Grass

Purple Fountain Grass

Purple Fountain Grass (*Pennisetum setaceum* 'Rubrum'), usually grown as an annual in northern counties, forming waist- or knee-high or taller clumps of fine-textured foliage with long, narrow, cylindrical "fox tail" flower heads. There are several other great fountain grasses, some of which are invasive.

Purple Muhly Grass

Purple Muhly Grass (*Muhlenbergia cappillaris*), an outstanding knee-high clump of slender foliage, is not much to look at until late summer and fall when it's covered with airy, billowy masses of striking pinkish red flowers. Hair grass (M. *dumosa*) is a billowy, light green clump up to seven feet tall, looking like a very fine, non-spreading bamboo.

River Oats

River Oats (*Chasmanthium latifolium*) is a native inland cousin of sea oats, with stiff, knee-high, narrow, wiry, bamboo-like stems. Topped with numerous arching flower stalks with two dozen or more dangling florets that have been compared to little fish or even "flattened armadillos." The stems hold up very well in dried arrangements. River oats, which tolerates a good bit of shade, can self-seed to the point of being invasive.

Striped Cane (*Arundo donax* 'Variegata') is for large gardens and screening only. It has very tall stems of coarse foliage that starts out variegated but turns to all-green by late summer; flowering stems may get twelve or more feet tall. May be too aggressive for small gardens and is considered an invasive exotic species in some states; needs room to spread slowly by tough rhizomes.

Striped Cane

Other Good Grasses:

Carex and **Acorus species** (*Carex* and *Acorus* species) are not true grasses, but are often used as edging, or small specimens, similar to Aztec grass (*Ophiopogon intermedius*). There are many highly variable cultivars, including gold and variegated forms.

Carex

Maiden Grass (*Miscanthus sinensis*) has many very interesting cultivars, but is limited to the northern half of the state. Dozens of tall flower stems open as tassels and gradually expand into soft feathery plumes in late summer and fall. Best cultivars include 'Cosmopolitan', 'Gracillimus', 'Strictus' (porcupine grass, with narrow, erect leaves with creamy stripes that run across the leaves), and compact 'Yaku Jima'.

Maiden Grass

Purple Love Grass (*Eragrostis spectabilis*) is one of Florida's most attractive small-clump grasses, two feet high with reddish fall color. Outstanding in groundcover masses.

Purple Love Grass

Ribbon Grass

Ribbon Grass (*Phalaris arundinacea*) is a fairly aggressive creeping groundcover to two or more feet high; a good border plant or "skirt" for shrubbery. Turns brown at first frost in North and Central Florida. 'Picta' has white-striped leaves.

 **Best for Beginners:**

- *Clump-Forming Bamboos*
- *Lemon Grass*
- *Pampas Grass*
- *Purple Fountain Grass*
- *River Oats*
- *Sand Cordgrass*

Kinda Tricky:

- *Running Bamboos*
- *Miscanthus* (not for South Florida)
- *Striped Cane* (large)
- *Wire Grass* (invasive)

Wire Grass (*Aristida stricta*) is the perfect grass for naturalizing in meadow plantings where soil is very poor. It is a silvery-green, foot or so tall, bunch-type grass best used in open spaces as a groundcover or with wildflowers.

You Might Be a Florida Gardener If...

- Five inches of rainfall one afternoon only means you won't have to water for a few days.
- There's no income tax, but the humidity is so thick you can lick it.
- Down South means the Keys.
- Your trench edging fills in with sand after every rain, and weeds instantly fill the gaps.
- Your hostas melted during their first seventy-five-degree night
- You have ever been "stung" by a poisonous moth larvae.
- Forty degrees is considered biting cold and more miserable than mosquitoes at ninety.
- You are fascinated by a standoff between a lizard and a "lubber" grasshopper.
- You grow a vine on a hurricane evacuation route sign.
- You call the stretch of beaches west of Apalachicola the Redneck Riviera.
- You personally know someone who has run over an armadillo.
- You grow at least one insect-eating plant.
- Your bumper sticker says "I Brake for Orchids."

- There is at least one vinyl manatee or alligator mailbox on your street.
- You garden in flip-flops so you can feel the fire ants quicker.
- You have posted by your phone the number to call if an alligator gets in your pool.
- You love summer because the vacationers have left and you can actually find a parking spot at a restaurant.
- You have ever tried to mimic the sound of a toad or tree frog.
- You know how many bags of compost your car can hold.
- You can amuse yourself for an hour with a garden hose.
- You have ever cleaned your car with a leaf blower.
- You carry a small stick to go pick up the newspaper, to keep spider webs off your face.
- You can grow prickly pear and palmettos side by side.
- Your worst natural disasters come with a televised "heads up" on the weather channel.
- All you want for your birthday is a new screen house.

Groundcovers
WITH GRIT

The lawn is not the only low-growing, spreading plant for the land-scape—there are dozens of "groundcovering" alternatives that not only look good all year, but are incredibly low maintenance.

Using groundcover plants has become the biggest trend in landscaping, replacing the wall to wall carpet of high maintenance turfgrass with its task-master demands on our precious time, water, energy, and pocketbooks, and its pest problems. In fact, for over twenty years university horticulturists have considered the excesses of large lawns a landscape liability, and publicly called those who over-water, over-feed, and over-spray their turf "environmental offenders." Strong words, but pretty much on target.

In practical terms, there are many situations where turfgrass is simply not workable or practical. In older neighborhoods with mature trees and large shrubs, even St. Augustine grass has a hard time getting enough sunlight to continue reproducing itself, and it gradually peters out or fades under the pressures of insects, diseases, or bad weather. Some large areas are too difficult to water often enough, so drought-tolerant weeds take over and have to be mowed more often than the grass itself. Even bahiagrass, one of the lowest-maintenance turfgrasses around, looks kinda weedy with its many seedheads.

Groundcovers, like a neat lawn area, can create strong "unity" in the landscape by visually tying plants, buildings, and other elements together in a smooth flow. And they often grow taller than lawn weeds, shading them out—which is very handy! Depending on the type you plant, other ways ground-covers are useful include:

- In densely shaded areas.
- To cover dry or sandy spots, even on salt-laden beach areas.
- To compete with and hide surface tree roots.
- To fill in difficult-to-mow areas between shrubs, trees, and paved areas.
- In parking lot or boulevard strips since they tolerate the intense heat and sun.
- As a cascading element in large container plantings.
- As a foot traffic barrier.

- To absorb rainfall run-off from buildings and paved areas.
- To provide interest with year-round foliage texture, and seasonal flower color.

Depending on what kind you choose, how it is planted, and how closely spaced new plants are, it may take a year or two, perhaps even longer, to get a groundcover to fill in and be relatively weed-free. An organic mulch such as shredded bark not only dramatically helps the appearance of a new groundcover area, but also shades the soil to help groundcover roots get established quickly, smothers many weed seeds, and feeds the soil as it decomposes.

When buying groundcover plants, make sure they are well rooted. Some, including monkey grass, mondo grass, and ferns can be cut into smaller plants to make your groundcover dollars go farther. You can also plant a few one year, then gradually expand your plantings by dividing them the next year. Water groundcovers as needed—a good soaking every now and then is much better than frequent light sprinklings—and fertilize lightly with an all-purpose fertilizer once or twice a year.

 Best for Beginners:

- *Asiatic Jasmine*
- *Cast-Iron Plant*
- *Coontie*
- *Liriope*
- *Mondo Grass*

Kinda Tricky:

- *Ajuga*
- *Ivy (grows too well)*
- *Junipers (mites and rust disease if overwatered)*

Viva la Difference!

Asiatic jasmine has small, pointy, glossy green leaves. So do hollies. If you plant them together, they end up running together visually, so no one can tell where one starts and the other begins. It is best to mix up leaf shapes and colors for more contrast. Ivy, with its big star-shaped leaves, contrasts with finer-textured ferns, or with large, bold-textured gingers or elephant's ears. Plant variegated groundcovers with solid-green shrubs, or vice versa.

Ardisia
Ardisia japonica
Shade or part shade

Unlike the upright, more shrubby coral ardisia (*A. crenata* or *A. crispa*), which is a highly-invasive plant on the "not recommended" list, Japanese ardisia is a sturdy, spreading groundcover for the shade.

FLOWER: Not very showy white flowers in the fall, followed by red berries in winter and spring.

PLANT: Low-growing, coarse-leaf plant to a foot or so high, spreads somewhat aggressively with underground runners. Leathery, bright green new leaves fade to duller olive green. Can crowd out many weeds.

INTERESTING KINDS: 'Hakuokan' has heavily variegated leaves with white on the edges; 'Amanogawa' has bright red berries and green leaves centered with gold.

Asiatic Jasmine
Trachelospermum asiaticum
Sun or part sun

One of the very best groundcovers for sun or shade, this popular vine can be clipped into tight mats or allowed to flow irregularly. It covers quickly and tolerates mild herbicides (used to kill intruding weeds).

FLOWER: Small fragrant white flowers are inconspicuous and hidden in the foliage.

PLANT: Thin but vigorous self-branching vine has many small, pointed, glossy green leaves. It is such a rapid grower that its edges have to be clipped regularly to keep it from overtaking sidewalks. Can climb shrubs or small trees. Roots readily in the summer.

INTERESTING KINDS: 'Minima' is a popular dwarf from. 'Bronze Beauty' has reddish new growth. 'Variegatum' is a choice groundcover for shade with creamy white blotches. 'Tricolor' with pink tinges was a Florida Plant of the Year in 2001.

Aztec Grass

Ophiopogon intermedius 'Argenteomarginatus'

Part sun or shade

Larger and more vigorous than "regular" mondo grass, the variegated, twelve- to eighteen-inch-tall clumps spread widely and aggressively as a brilliant groundcover for difficult, dry settings. Very useful for areas under shrubs or large trees, or mass-planted in shaded areas.

FLOWER: Small stems produce white flowers then black fruits in the summer, often hidden among the leaves.

PLANT: Many thin, arching green leaves with yellowish white edges are produced in clumps that spread outward to form thick mats. Very easy to divide and spread around for expanded plantings.

INTERESTING KINDS: No varieties that I know of.

Beach Sunflower

Helianthus debilis

Sun

This native plant grows well in all parts of Florida, especially in hot, sandy soils that get little or no irrigation. It is a "must" for dune stabilization, and is ideal around the base of a mailbox. Tolerates intense radiated heat from sidewalks or pavement.

FLOWER: Showy yellow sunflowers, two inches across, with dark centers; produced all summer and fall.

PLANT: Low-growing, spreading mass of dull green leaves, forms a mound up to two feet tall and twice that wide. Thrives on neglect.

INTERESTING KINDS: No cultivars that I am aware of.

Cast-Iron Plant
Aspidistra elatior
Dense to part shade

The name says it all—this common old-garden plant, tough enough to grow under live oaks, is a mainstay of shaded gardens; it can sunscald even in winter sun. It is an excellent container plant on a shaded porch or patio.

FLOWER: Insignificant lilac or greenish brown bell-shaped flowers borne on very short stems in the spring, hidden by the tall foliage.

PLANT: Pointed spearheads of deep, forest-green leaves to two or three feet tall and four inches or more wide arise once a year in the late winter and early spring from clumps of roots and persist until the following year.

INTERESTING KINDS: 'Variegata' has irregular-width streaks of pale yellow, 'Milky Way' has lots of white spots on green leaves

Chocolate Soldiers
Pseuderanthemum alatum
Shade or part sun

This shade-loving gem is so easy to grow, and spreads so well from seed, it is sometimes considered a weed—but it is a delightful mainstay of the shade garden, though hard to find in nurseries (get a start from another gardener, who will have lots to share).

FLOWER: Spikes of bright rose-lavender flowers in the spring are held above the foliage on long stalks; seeds disperse with a snap of the seedpod.

PLANT: Hand-sized, oval leaves are an unusual medium to light brown, each with a metallic silver pattern in the center. It is a stunning contrast to variegated or darker green plants, or those with yellow flowers.

INTERESTING KINDS: None other than the species.

Creeping Juniper
Juniperus species
Sun to part sun

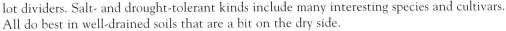

Among the toughest evergreens for sunny, harsh growing conditions including parking lot dividers. Salt- and drought-tolerant kinds include many interesting species and cultivars. All do best in well-drained soils that are a bit on the dry side.

FLOWER: Not noticeable, but occasionally displays blue berries in winter.

PLANT: Spreading evergreens with small, prickly green or blue-green needle-like leaves. Grows from under six inches to two feet high, extending several feet in every direction. Some have plum- or purple-tinged winter foliage.

INTERESTING KINDS: Dwarf shore (grows to twelve inches high), 'Prince of Wales' (eight inches), Parson's (eighteen inches), blue rug (four inches), dwarf Japanese garden (one foot) 'Andorra' (two feet) (some are more susceptible to spider mites and leaf blights) and others.

Dwarf Mexican Petunia
Ruellia brittoniana 'Katie'
Sun, part sun, shade

Though much smaller than the more invasive species form, this tight little clump makes up for its size with a powerful punch of foliage and flowers, for sun or shade.

FLOWER: Papery, five-petaled, petunia-like flowers up to two inches across in purple, lavender-pink, or white all summer and fall. Each opens in the morning and sheds cleanly that evening.
PLANT: Tidy eight- or ten-inch clump of narrow, dark-green leaves that spreads slowly, unlike the taller kinds. Easy to propagate by rooting divisions.

INTERESTING KINDS: 'Katie' has purple-blue flowers; 'Colobe Pink' has pink flowers; 'Strawberries and Cream' has lavender blossoms and white-speckled leaves.

Ferns
All sorts of weird Latin names
Shade

Ferns are a "given" as groundcovers for the shade. Most are spreading, with feathery fronds, and many are evergreen throughout all but the northern counties of Florida. There are many, many great ferns, but the ones listed below are considered among the toughest and most commonly available in all parts of Florida.

Autumn Fern

Autumn Fern (*Dryopteris erythrosora*), named a Florida Plant of the Year in 1998, is a clumping evergreen to two feet tall whose new growth is reddish bronze.

Cinnamon Fern (*Osmunda cinnamomea*) gets up to five feet tall with fertile fronds dusted with cinnamon-like spores. Fronds turn golden yellow or orange in the fall before going dormant.

Cinnamon Fern

Holly Fern

Holly Fern (*Cyrtomium falcatum*) is a dark green, bushel-basket-size fern with large, glossy, leathery leaves (like holly leaves) that requires dense shade—it will burn even in winter sunshine.

Leatherleaf Fern (*Rumohra adiantiformis*) has upright, evergreen foliage up to three feet tall, with fronds stiff enough for florists to use.

Pineland Brake Fern (*Pteris bahamensis*) is a native fern with airy fronds of narrow leaflets.

Southern Wood Fern (*Dryopteris ludoviciana*) is a very popular, fast-spreading native deciduous fern with light green foliage to three feet tall. Spreads by rhizomes.

Sword Fern (*Nephrolepis exaltata*), whose most famous selection is the Boston fern, is fast growing to two feet high with bright green fluffy foliage that goes dormant in northern counties.

West Indian Holly Fern (*Arachnoides simplicor* 'Variegata') is evergreen, with deeply cut, dark green fronds whose segments each have a creamy yellow center stripe.

Smothering the Lawn

One of the easiest ways to lose a large area of grass is to simply smother it. Cover the area with flattened-out cardboard boxes, cover them with grass clippings, compost, and mulch, and it instantly looks pretty good, just like a large mulched area. And within just a few weeks the grass underneath is not only dead, but also decomposing (along with the cover material) into some pretty decent soil. You can plant groundcovers right through the covering material and, as the grass roots decompose, they provide nutrient-rich "paths" for the new groundcover roots. This is a real timesaver for folks trying to lose part of the lawn before planting groundcovers.

Firecracker Plant
Russelia equisetiformis
Sun or light shade

Normally thought of as a small shrub, this cascading willowy mass of foliage and flowers can spread through an area with suckering underground stems, becoming a spectacular groundcover. Use it where it can be seen from below, such as flowing over a retaining wall, down a slope, or as a specimen in a large flower pot.

FLOWER: Showy red tubular flowers over an inch long resemble firecrackers. Produced during the entire warm season.

PLANT: Arching, cascading branches of very thin, wire-like, nearly leafless green stems that branch repeatedly. Evergreen in all but the most northern counties of Florida, where it needs pruning back after a hard freeze.

INTERESTING KINDS: A yellow-flowering form is available.

Ivy
Hedera species
Shade or part shade

Both English ivy (*H. helix*) and the faster-growing, larger-leaf Algerian ivy (*H. canariensis*) are popular vines used for extensive groundcovers in shaded areas. In some cases, they completely replace the need for grass. They can climb trees and walls using stem roots, and can develop leaf spot or root rot problems if watered too often. Spider mites and scale can be problems, especially if the ivy is grown in full sun.

FLOWER: Mature plants have small white flowers and black berries. Not very showy.

PLANT: Rapidly-spreading, self-branching woody vine covered with deeply-lobed palmate leaves in solid green or variegated.

INTERESTING KINDS: Variegated Algerian ivy has lighter green and creamy white blotches on leaves; there are many dozens of interesting English ivy cultivars for container gardening.

Mondo Grass

Ophiopogon japonicus

Dense shade to part sun

Mondo or "little monkey grass" is a deep green grassy groundcover that spreads aggressively in the densest shade, even under live oaks and evergreen shrubs. Use as a border or as an evergreen lawn substitute.

FLOWER: Inconspicuous spikes of pinkish white, bell-shaped flowers held close to the ground, usually hidden in the foliage but visible if mondo is mowed in the spring. It also has light blue berries.

PLANT: Low-growing, arching, fine-textured (thin) leaves that are very dark green, produced in soft clumps that spread rapidly by way of runners that can extend six inches or more from the "mother" plants before sprouting the following spring.

INTERESTING KINDS: 'Nana' is a very small, tight ball of foliage under four inches tall. 'Nigrescens' is slow spreading and nearly black.

Monkey Grass or Lily Turf

Liriope species

Heavy shade to moderate sun

This is the border plant of choice for dry shade gardens, but also makes a superb addition to container plantings.

FLOWER: Summer stalks of small, hyacinth-like, blue, pinkish lavender, or sometimes white flowers, excellent for flower arrangements. Blue-black berries persist into fall.

PLANT: Narrow, grassy foliage a foot or so tall is evergreen. *Liriope muscari* is outstanding as a dense border plant or shade perennial; *L. spicata* has narrower leaves and spreads rapidly as a shady groundcover.

INTERESTING KINDS: 'Evergreen Giant' and 'Variegata' are very popular forms; 'Monroe White' has white flowers and 'Silvery Sunproof' does best in sun, but its white variegation turns yellow in the shade.

Moses-in-the-Cradle
Tradescantia spathacea
Sun or shade

Talk about tough—this little perennial, also known as dwarf oyster plant, which spreads quite readily (but is not as weedy as the related tall oyster plant on the invasive plants list), will grow in the crack of a tombstone! It prospers under any conditions.

FLOWER: Small white three-petaled flowers are held in little half-open "canoe" shaped bracts (hence the common name).

PLANT: Upright rosettes up to a foot or more tall and wide of sword-shaped leaves that are green on the upper side, purple-burgundy on the underside. Plants grow into thick colonies. Easy to propagate by division.

INTERESTING KINDS: 'Variegata' has leaves striped in red and yellowish green.

New Gold Lantana
Lantana camara 'New Gold'
Sun or part shade

Most lantanas are invasive thugs in Florida, spreading everywhere by seed (which are deadly toxic, by the way). The cultivar 'New Gold' (also called 'Gold Mound') is essentially sterile so produces very few if any seeds, and it's just as attractive to butterflies.

FLOWER: Small but very showy clusters of short tubular flowers, produced at the ends of new growth during the entire spring, summer, and fall.

PLANT: Wiry, self-branching stems shoot off a central trunk close to the ground, with toothed, pointy-oval leaves having a peculiar pungent scent when crushed.

INTERESTING KINDS: Other popular, fruitless groundcover lantanas include pink and cream 'Pinkie', orange red 'Spreading Sunset', and 'Lemon Swirl' with a yellow band around each leaf. Trailing lantana (*L. montevidensis*) is a spreading, ground-hugging mat of lavender or white flowers. Pineland lantana is a native Florida species, non-invasive, with pale yellow flowers.

Peacock Ginger
Kaempferia species
Shade

Selected as a Florida Plant of the Year in 1998, this exotic shade-loving groundcover spreads into a low mat of oval or rounded, decorative leaves punctuated with bright flowers all summer and fall.

FLOWER: An inch or more wide, African violet-like flowers, can be white, pink, or lavender, often with a purple spot on one lip and fragrant, are produced just above the foliage on stiff stems in the summer and fall.

PLANT: Flat masses of leaves six or more inches long and nearly as wide, usually with a peacock-feather iridescence of bronze and green, or silvery streaks and zoning, sometimes with purplish undersides. Spreads by rhizomes or tubers.

INTERESTING KINDS: Several species available, each equally interesting. Variegated peacock lily (*K. gilbertii*) has narrow leaves with white margins and stripes.

Perennial Peanut
Arachis glabrata
Sun

A Florida Plant of the Year selection in 2002, this low-growing, dense plant spreads like nothing else, and though it looks delicate it is durable enough to be walked on. It is well adapted to the dry, infertile sands of Florida, and, being in the pea family, it even makes its own fertilizer!

FLOWER: Yellow pea-like flowers in the summer are edible, and taste like peanuts.

PLANT: Spreading mass of small, three-leaflet foliage that tolerates intolerable drought and low fertility. An outstanding lawn substitute that takes radiated heat from sidewalks.

INTERESTING KINDS: 'Florigraze' and 'Arbrook' are commercial forage cultivars, used for grazing cattle, goats, rabbits, etc. The kind used by gardeners for a groundcover is generally sold as 'Ecoturf'.

Purple Heart
Tradescantia pallida
Sun or light shade

Intense conditions call for intense plants. The nearly gaudy purple-red foliage of this sturdy spreading plant belies its toughness—it will grow just as well in traffic medians from Highway 1 in south Miami to the streets of Pensacola! Easy to propagate, this heirloom belongs in every Florida garden as a groundcover or spreading potted plant.

FLOWER: Fairly showy half-inch-wide pink flowers with three petals stand out against the backdrop of foliage.

PLANT: Spreading foot-tall mass of pointed, finger-like purple-red leaves that are squeaky slick to the touch.

INTERESTING KINDS: 'Purple Queen' is also a common name. It is a close relative to wandering Jew, but is bolder and much hardier.

Society Garlic
Tulbaghia violacea
Sun or light shade

The aromatic leaves of this clump-forming bulb are very garlicky, and can actually be used for culinary purposes. It is mass-planted as a groundcover in sometimes harsh conditions that include drought and radiated heat from walls.

FLOWER: Airy round balls of up to twenty pink, white, or lilac flowers are held high above foliage on slender, two-foot stalks in the spring, summer, and fall.

PLANT: Evergreen, upright mass of slender, bluish-green leaves that form dense mounds that can be divided at any time.

INTERESTING KINDS: 'Variegata' has a creamy stripe down the center of each leaf. 'Tricolor' has leaves with white edges with a pinkish cast that intensifies in cool weather. 'Silver Lace' has leaves edged in white.

Other Good Groundcovers:

Bugle Weed or **Carpet Bugle** (*Ajuga reptans*) is a very popular groundcover for shaded gardens, with flat rosettes of sometimes-colorful leaves and spikes of blue spring flowers, but it is disease-prone in South Florida, and very susceptible to nematode injury.

Calathea (*Calathea* species) has several species with beautifully patterned foliage for deep shade. Surprisingly hardy in even the northern counties of Florida.

Dancing Girls (*Globba* species) is a shade-loving ginger relative with bright green sheaths of leaves and long, arching sprays of often brilliantly colored bracts.

Foxtail Asparagus Fern (*Asparagus densiflorus* 'Meyerii') is neither a true fern (ferns never flower), nor true edible asparagus (which has spreading rhizomes). This drought-hardy, fluffy evergreen is excellent for mass planting or container culture.

Matted St. John's Wort (*Hypericum reductum*) is a full-sun, sand-and-drought-loving native with evergreen needle-like leaves and yellow flowers. It gets a foot or so tall and four feet wide.

Nippon Lily (*Rohdea japonica*) is like a tough, short cast-iron plant with spikes of showy red fruit in the winter; can grow under evergreen holly trees and magnolias.

Pennywort (*Dichondra carolinensis*), though native, is often seen as a weed in the lawn, but with its vigorous growth and tidy, smooth, round leaves, it makes a superb groundcover or lawn substitute where it is encouraged.

Quailberry or Christmas Berry (*Rossopetalum illicifolium*) is a shrubby little holly-like groundcover with spiny tough leaves that almost glow red and orange when new, and red berries. It needs no water once established.

Railroad Vine (*Ipomoea pes-caprae*) is a native, extremely salt tolerant vine that makes a good dune plant. It has brilliant purple flowers in the spring and fall.

Sedum (*Sedum acre*) is a succulent with densely branching stems covered with tiny, narrow, pale green leaves and showy stalks of bright yellow flowers in the spring.

Sunshine Mimosa (*Mimosa strigilosa*) is an oddball Florida native sometimes seen as a weed, but it makes an interesting groundcover for sunny, poor soils. Its foliage and flowers are pretty enough, but the way its leaves fold up when they are touched or disturbed is fascinating.

Wedelia (*Wedelia trilobata*) is such an aggressive groundcover in even very dry conditions, it has been placed on the invasive plants list. It has showy yellow flowers most of the season.

Wintercreeper (*Euonymus fortunei*) is a sturdy evergreen vine that, though susceptible to leaf diseases and scale, can be pruned easily into a fast, sturdy groundcover. Some kinds have variegated foliage. Wintercreeper grows best in north Florida.

Other plants in this book that are used as groundcovers include: creeping fig, other ferns, dwarf gardenia, spiderwort, spider plant, wild petunia, kalanchoe, variegated dwarf bamboo, certain bromeliads (*Guzmania*, *Aechmea* 'Silver Vase'), gingers (pinecone, pineapple, hidden), peperomia, coreopsis, and spreading annuals such as dwarf porterweed, blue daze, petunias, wandering Jew, and jewels of Opar.

Mama Said Not to Say "Thank You"

No gardener plies his or her hobby alone, at least not completely. Every time we plant something—unless it is a wildflower that just appears from the hand of Nature—we are sharing the legacy of gardeners gone before. Whether the plant was grown by a commercial horticulturist, or passed along from garden to garden over many generations, we are touching other gardeners.

Folks who sell plants try hard to predict what gardeners want—the rule of thumb in commercial horticulture is *what you don't sell, you got to smell*. On the other hand, gardeners who share are more direct—nobody wants a plant that is hard to grow, or blighted by pests, so what gets shared has already been garden-tested.

By the way, when you get a plant from another gardener, there are two ways of showing appreciation. One is to simply thank the gardener, which is polite. But very often, especially in the South, the giver will say "Oh, no—don't thank me or it won't grow."

You think I'm making this up? In my lectures I often ask if anyone has ever heard that response; in the South, it's usually a majority of the audience, but in other parts of the country it is mostly just those who were raised by a Southern gardener.

The way I was taught, is to say "Mama said not to thank you for this, or it won't grow." That's the exact way I say it. If I get a quizzical look, I follow it up with "But thanks, I appreciate it!" But if you get a "That's right, honey," in return, you know you and the gardener were raised well. A long time gardener once said "the best way to thank someone for a plant is to pass a piece along to someone else."

Works for me—plus it keeps what comes around, going around.

PROVEN
Palms

Pick out any Florida postcard—or watch any hurricane advisory—and it will likely have a palm in the photo. It's not only the state tree, it's a survivor of everything the climate can hurl at it.

Because they are used in nearly every imaginable landscape setting, from striking single specimen or naturalistic group accents, to street trees, hedges, and barriers, to comforting container beauties for both poolside and indoors, palms lend a tropical flair to all Florida gardens. Of the thirty or so different palms routinely offered in garden centers, only a dozen or so are tough enough to be used universally throughout Florida by both home gardeners and landscapers.

Container-grown palms can be set out any time, but field-grown kinds are best planted in the spring or summer when new root growth is at its peak (palms make little or no root growth in the fall or winter). Reduce transplant

shock with dug palms by removing most of the fronds at planting time. Brace tall palms with two or three boards until they get established, and keep them moist the first summer or two, after which they are generally very drought tolerant.

For best growth and vigor, and pest resistance, feed palms regularly, at least once or twice a year. Scatter a little fertilizer around the butt of each palm and water it in. Though palms usually get plenty of fertilizer from lawn food broadcast nearby, they really benefit from an occasional light feeding of commercial palm fertilizer, which is carefully crafted with extra nutrients, especially magnesium (which is why you sometimes hear about people putting Epsom salts around their palms). By the way, most mature palms "pull" nutrients from old fronds, so don't prune foliage until the stems have turned brown, if it doesn't drop off first (some palms are "self cleaning").

If you want to show off unique palms in striking poses all by themselves, they will need mulching (with natural bark, seashells, or white gravel). To protect their roots and butts from excess drying and string trimmer damage, underplant them with "skirt" plants. Easy plantings that don't require a lot of extra water include liriope, mondo grass, junipers, African iris, ruellia, plumbago, purple heart, Indian hawthorn, dwarf yaupon holly, ferns, ornamental grasses, and beach sunflower.

Best for Beginners:

- Coontie
- Fan Palm
- Jelly Palm
- Needle Palm
- Sago Palm
- Saw Palmetto
- Windmill Palm

Kinda Tricky:

- Areca Palm
- Bismarck Palm
- Canary Island Palm
- Chinese Fan Palm
- Washington Palm

(Because they get too big, they are susceptible to disease, or aren't cold hardy)

Cabbage Palm

Sabal palmetto

Full sun or part sun

Florida's official state tree is a sturdy native with tall, straight trunks to fifty or more feet tall whose leaves are commonly used for making baskets, hats, and thatched roofs. It grows well as a single specimen, but usually looks better when planted in a group, or as a screen or hedge. As older fronds drop naturally, they leave attractive bases. This palm's "heart" is edible, and can be sliced or shredded and cooked like cabbage.

Chinese Fan Palm

Livistona chinensis

Full sun or part sun

One of the least fussy palms, it is hardy to about 15 degrees; gardeners near the Georgia state line may need to protect it from a sudden deep freeze, or grow it as a container plant. Somewhat slow growing to about thirty feet tall, it has strikingly bright-green, rounded leaves up to six feet wide with drooping tips. Do not mulch this palm or it may be more susceptible to fungal attacks. Seeds are a pretty deep blue-green.

Coontie
Zamia pumila
Full sun or part sun

This very hardy Florida native is a cycad, not a true palm. It is a slow-growing, clump-forming plant with no real "trunk" but lots of dark green glossy leaves. It grows equally well in full sun or in shade, as interesting little foundation "shrubs", or massed like a groundcover. A very close relative, the cardboard palm (*Z. furfuracea*), has interesting broad leaflets but is freeze-sensitive; it makes makes a superb accent or groundcover in South and Central Florida, and an excellent, low-maintenance potted plant in northern counties.

Date Palm
Phoenix dactylifera
Full sun or part sun

This is the classic "desert oasis" palm, with tall trunks to seventy or eighty feet and long, slightly arching fronds of stiff, pointed leaflets. It often grows in small clumps with several trunks from basal suckers, and bears the "dates" you find in markets. The upper trunk is patterned with short stalks of old leaves. Date palms can recover from freezes into the lower teens. The Canary Island date palm (*P. canariensis*) has bright green leaves, but its crown is slow to recover from hard freezes in northern areas.

Dwarf Palmetto
Sabal minor
Full sun or part sun

Hardy to well below zero, the native dwarf palmetto is perfect for use as an understory shrub in shade, but can also hold up well in full sunlight.Its stout underground trunk sprouts large palmate leaves on long sturdy stems, often reac hing to eight or ten feet high and nearly as wide. It tolerates heavy wet soils.

European Fan Palm
Chamaerops humilis
Full sun or part sun

At ten to fifteen feet tall, this medium-height specimen palm is one of the best for general use. Its two-foot palmate fronds and stout, multi-stemmed clumping effect make it suitable as an accent, screen, or even potted plant for patios or decks in all parts of Florida. Petioles are armed with sharp teeth. A relatively low maintenance plant.

Jelly or Pindo Palm
Butia capitata
Full sun or part sun

Hardy to 5 degrees, this is one of Florida's finest landscape specimens, focal point, or street palms— one of the best for under power lines. It is slow-growingto up to about fifteen feet and can get almost as wide as it is tall, with arching, fernlike fronds. Some selectioons have somewhat blue-green leaves, and typically old stubs of leaf stalks can persist for years. Bright yellow, orange, or red fruits are edible and can be made into jelly.

Needle Palm
Rhapidophyllum hystrix
Full sun or part sun

Similar in appearance to the coarser dwarf palmetto, this native palm, which was selected as a Florida Plant of the Year in 2004, is very slow growing and low, up to eight or so feet tall and nearly as wide, with dark green palmate leaves. It is a very good palm for use as an understory plant in the shade, or massing around foundations of buildings, or even for erosion control, including in northern Florida where it can tolerate well below zero degrees. It has long, very sharp spines on its trunk, hence the common name of needle palm.

Sago

Cycas revoluta
Full sun or part sun

Not a true palm, this dinosaur-era relative has long been very popular for accents, foundation plantings, and containers. Deep green, glossy foliage is produced all at once in a fountain around a center "cone" that is either male of female; orange fruits are very attractive. Multiple "pups" growing around the main plant give a fuller effect. **Note:** Serious, nearly incurable scale insect infestations have recently killed many sagos in Florida. Check with your Extension Service office for the latest recommendations.

Saw Palmetto

Serenoa repens
Full sun or part sun

Another hardy native, this small clump-forming palm only gets around six or so feet tall and wide, and is perfectly adapted to all Florida soil types. Though its starkly divided palmate leaves have very sharp "needles" on the tips of each petiole, the plant still makes an excellent accent plant beside patios and along walks. They are almost always planted in small groups. The silver-blue form 'Cinerea' is much preferred by landscapers and home gardeners alike.

Washington Palm
Washingtonia robusta
Full sun or part sun

Sometimes called Mexican fan palm, this fast-growing, single-trunk giant can reach eighty to ninety feet, quickly outgrowing its space in a typical home landscape (and often making it susceptible to lightening strikes!). The flowers are showy creamy white, and overlapping old leaf stalks give the trunk an interesting pattern, and provide a place for ferns, bromeliads, and other plants to grow. It is hardy to well below freezing but is pest sensitive. Old leaves fall against the trunk in a hula skirt effect.

Windmill Palm
Trachycarpus fortunei
Full sun or part sun

Hardy to 10 degrees below zero, this is perhaps the hardiest palm of all—even north of Atlanta, Georgia, when protected. This single-trunk palm has bright green, palmate fronds that are divided almost to their base, and tips that droop. Its trunk is covered with dense brown fibers, giving a hairy texture. Used most commonly as a specimen or accent plant either in the ground or in planters, it has a moderately fast growth rate and can eventually reach twenty, thirty, or more feet tall.

Other palms that are freeze-sensitive but suitable for Central and South Florida:

Areca Palm

Areca Palm (*Dypsis lutescens*) is very popular outdoors in South Florida, and one of the most popular indoor or potted palms elsewhere. Arching, feather-like foliage, with a golden crown shaft and leaf bases. It makes a thick clump. Fertilize often to keep it green.

Bismarck Palm (*Bismarckia nobilis*) is one of the coolest palms of all, with huge, distinctly blue-green leaves and somewhat showy maroon and white flowers. Unfortunately, it is hardy only in Central and South Florida, but can be enjoyed as a container palm elsewhere.

Blue Latania Palm (*Latania loddigesii*) has a very stately appearance, having accordion-like pleats in its large, blue-gray leaves. The plant is not as large as the hardier, blue Bismarck palm.

Blue Latania Palm

Hurricane Palm (*Dictyosperma album*) is named for its ability to tolerate extreme winds. Its long fronds include a sturdy mid rib that holds thin leaflets in place. Excellent specimen or street palm.

Lady Palm

Lady Palm (*Rhapis* species) is a very slender, upright, small palm that grows slowly to twelve or fourteen feet tall, topped with small, graceful, deeply-divided palmate fronds. There is a variegated form. It is very shade tolerant.

Paurotis Palm (*Acoelorrhaphe wrightii*) is a medium-height Florida native, one of the few that will grow well in wet soils. It forms a multi-trunk specimen that can be used for screening. Petioles on the palmate fronds are armed with sharp teeth, and its showy yellow flowers produce attractive black fruit. Borderline hardy in North Florida.

Ruffled Fan Palm (*Licuala grandis*) is perhaps the most stunning palm for its huge, round, bright green, pleated leaves that wave in the slightest breeze from atop slender, short trunks.

DISEASES OF PALMS—especially one called "lethal yellows"—can be more serious on some palms than others. Other diseases can enter trunks that have been hit with a string trimmer. Check with your county Extension Service office for recommendations for prevention or control.

Blow, Winds, Blow

Californians have earthquake epicenters, Northerners have blizzard whiteouts, Floridians have hurricanes, which treat the landscape like a giant garden Etch-a-Sketch. Heavy rains often do more damage than blowing winds, and losing power in summer and fall humidity are more than an inconvenience—especially after days on end of hearing the next installment of "total weather coverage" and endless repetition of words and phrases like "feeder bands," "tornadic activity," "swaths," and—perhaps the worst—"hunker down." It can drive sane people nuts. Oh, and "low lying area." To determine whether you live in a low-lying area, look at your driver's license; if it says Florida, you live in a low-lying area.

Having been through hurricanes in three Gulf Coast states, I have some suggestions for preparedness, starting with the most practical three-step approach: Buy enough food and bottled water to last your family for at least four days, put these supplies into your car, then drive to Indiana and don't come back until after Thanksgiving. If this doesn't fit your plan, here are some easy guidelines I have picked up from various sources, or observed outright:

- First of all, keep in mind that it only takes a sixty-mile-per-hour wind to rip a coconut from a palm and hurl it twenty miles like a cannonball.
- If they are predicting a Category 1 hurricane, leave the pots outside. Category 2, bring in the small containers. Category 3, bring in everything you can carry—what you leave outside is a potential missile (even the outdoor grill and visiting relatives).
- Seriously, if you live in Florida, get a good chainsaw, and if you have a backup generator, run it a few minutes every month or so to keep it from gumming up from disuse. Keep these staples for power outages—portable camp stove, bottled water, canned goods (with an opener!), batteries, etc.—you know the drill, but if you don't actually do it, you're at risk of doing without.

See you in Indiana.

Perennials
THAT PREVAIL

Perennials—generally herbaceous plants that live three or more years—are "hot" in Florida gardens, partly because many of them will grow without any care to speak of, and partly because the nursery and landscape industry has started promoting them more.

Unfortunately, many popular perennial plants from other parts of the country—peonies and astilbe come to mind—simply cannot survive the warm, humid climate in Florida; on the other hand, it's easy to grow astounding tropical perennials that have to be treated as potted plants elsewhere. It's a good swap, and this chapter highlights a few dozen of the most well adapted plants for Florida's climate.

Site Selection and Soil Preparation

Although some perennials, such as ferns and gingers, tolerate heavy shade, many others bloom best with at least half a day of sunshine. Both good soil drainage and air circulation are very important for avoiding root and foliage diseases. Soil preparation for perennials is similar to that for annuals; do it well at the beginning, because perennials may grow there for years with little opportunity for you to correct any problems. Add organic matter such as bark, peat, or compost (or a combination of several types) to soils to help with drainage and hold nutrients during rainy spells, and to hold moisture during dry spells. A layer of organic matter two or three inches deep, worked into the soil a shovel's depth, is usually adequate, and "feeds" the soil as it decomposes.

Planting and Care

Set perennial plants level with or slightly higher than the soil around them, and completely cover roots without burying the stem or crown. Water thoroughly to settle the soil; then mulch the bed surface to keep the soil from drying, crusting, and overheating in the summer and to prevent many weed seeds from germinating. If you do not mulch your plants, lightly work up the soil surface in the spring to break and aerate compacted soils. This also helps water penetration and makes it easier to incorporate fertilizer.

Perennials need a balance of several nutrients; most garden supply stores carry a wide variety of fertilizer mixes. Slow-acting kinds are easier to use and better for plants than fast-acting liquids or generic garden fertilizers. Apply fertilizers sparingly to plants early in their growing season, after new growth begins to show. If plants are growing well, no additional fertilizer may be needed; otherwise, a second light feeding will be helpful several weeks into the season. The main things to remember about feeding perennials are that a little is better than a lot, and too much is worse than none at all.

Make sure all plants in the same area have the same basic soil, sun, and watering needs. For best effect, contrast plants by foliage shape or color, or use a simple, bold combination of "spiky" plants, "roundy" plants, and "frilly" plants. If needed, add a hard feature such as statue, birdbath, bench, or artwork to create a year-round scene.

Take a little extra care to choose and plant perennials well, followed with mulch, and occasional feeding and watering, and their lives and performance will be greatly extended.

Propagation

Most gardeners find that digging and separating plants—giving each piece its own portion of stem and roots—takes very little expertise; first practice on monkey grass and daylilies for experience, and before long you will have the hang of it. Though some perennials can be divided any time you feel like it, in general it is best to do it during their dormant or "off" season; divide spring bloomers in the fall and fall bloomers in spring. The worst time to divide is when they are in full bloom.

Quite a few perennial plants can be rooted from stem cuttings, choosing stems that are mature and firm but not yet hardened and woody. Cut off four- to six-inch segments, pinch off the succulent tip and any flower buds, and remove lower leaves that will be below the surface of the potting soil. Root in pots of a porous, well-drained rooting medium, such as equal parts sand, perlite, and peat moss, watering daily or as needed. Rooting usually happens within three or four weeks.

African Bush Daisy

Gamolepis chrysanthemoides

Sun

Bush daisies are tidy mounds of fine-textured foliage that produce cheerful flowers all year in South Florida, and through the warm season in northern counties. It is used massed or in small groups in tight spaces like between sidewalks and curbs.

FLOWER: Yellow daisies are produced year-round in most of Florida. Can reseed into nearby areas, but is easy to control.

PLANT: Mounding mass two to four feet or more high and three to five feet wide, dense with deeply-divided, ferny leaves. Requires well-drained soils.

INTERESTING KINDS: Bush daisy (*Euryops pectinatus*) is very similar except a little larger with grayish leaves. Very tolerant of seacoast conditions, including high winds. 'Viridis' has deep green leaves; 'Munchkin' is compact to only about three feet tall and a little wider.

Angelonia

Angelonia angustifolia

Sun

Often sold as an annual in the rest of the country, this upright shrubby plant is among the toughest summer perennials in Florida, blooming non-stop in very hot areas, including in containers on pavement.

FLOWER: Slender, showy spikes packed with purple, plum, pink, white, or multi-colored flowers very suitable as foot-long cut flowers. Cutting faded flowering stems promotes faster new flowering growth.

PLANT: Almost generic sprawling shrubby plant with many upright stems up to two or more feet tall.

INTERESTING KINDS: Blue-flowered 'Hilo Princess' was named one of the first Florida Plant of the Year selections in 1998. Members of the Angel Mist Series have flowers sometimes marked with white, pink, or purple. Those in the Carita Series branch close to the ground, giving a fuller look.

Angel's Trumpet

Brugmansia species

Sun or light shade

There are two kinds of angel's trumpet (*Brugmansia* and *Datura*), and both are showy, exotic, and interesting conversation plants sure to bring comments.

FLOWER: Long twisted buds open at dusk into large, flaring, trumpet-shaped flowers, usually very fragrant, that attract large hawk moths. May be white, pink, peach, yellow, golden, or even purple, double or single. Seedpods are interesting but seeds are poisonous if taken in large quantities.

PLANT: Upright treelike shrub with large oval pointed leaves. Herbaceous in northern counties and will be killed back by freezes.

INTERESTING KINDS: *Brugmansia* species in general have flowers that hang down; there are quite a lot of interesting cultivars in different colors. *Datura* species are lower-growing and spreading, like a thick groundcover, with upward-facing flowers and swollen, shiny seedpods; 'Cornucopia' has gorgeous double purple and white flowers.

Artemisia

Artemisia species

Full sun to light shade

Many perennials need a companion to help set them off. Few plants are as effective as grayish-white artemisia, especially when used as a "unifying element" in large beds.

FLOWER: Insignificant, usually not even noticed.

PLANT: Generally vigorous, bushy or spreading to two or three feet, with woody stems covered with silver gray or white leaves that are soft and pungent when broken. Some varieties are invasive; others simply flop over large areas and can be pruned severely.

INTERESTING KINDS: 'Silver King' is a common rhizomatous (invasive) variety, but the most popular "designer" type is 'Powis Castle', a fern-leaf hybrid that forms a dense, knee-high spreading mound whose long stems can extend to six feet, but which is easily tidied up by pruning.

Banana
Musa species
Full sun or light shade

Nothing says tropics more than bananas—not even palms. Wind- and cold-resistant types, dwarf varieties, and those with colorful leaves and flowers, make this a most interesting addition to any Florida garden.

FLOWER: Long, cascading clusters of female flowers looking like small bananas, and pollinating male flowers nearer the bottom, encased in a purple sheath. Fruiting varieties produce in bunches, with some being sweeter or firmer than others. Since it takes a year and a half for flowering and fruiting, a hard freeze that kills the plants back to the ground may cause the loss of that year's fruit.

PLANT: Slow-spreading clumps of large underground corms produce tall stalks of huge, waxy green leaves.

INTERESTING KINDS:

No two gardeners will agree on which is the best tasting banana for Florida gardens (mostly *Musa acuminata*), but the most popular include 'Cavendish', 'Dwarf Cavendish', 'Mysore' or "lady fingers", 'Goldfinger', 'Dwarf Brazilian', and 'Ice Cream' ('Blue Java'). 'Rojo' (several other names) has maroon stripes on the leaves and tiny, inedible dark maroon fruit. Ornamental species (M. × *paradisica*, *ornata*, *velutina*, others) have decorative leaves with purple, maroon, pink, or bronze colorations, and generally small, seedy fruit in showy bracts of pink or purple. The very popular banana relative, Abyssinian banana (*Ensete ventricosum* 'Maurelii", has totally red stems and leaves.

Chinese Lantern or Flowering Maple
Abutilon species and hybrids
Part shade

Used in the rest of the country as a "parlor" plant, this Florida-hardy perennial is one of the best hummingbird attractors around.

FLOWER: Continuous production of drooping bell-shaped flowers two to three inches across in red, yellow, orange, pink, or white, rich in nectar for hummingbirds.

PLANT: Upright, arching stems to eight or more feet tall, can be "pinched" for bushier growth. Leaves are maple-like, six or more inches across, often speckled or variegated. **Note:** Too much nitrogen fertilizer forces leafy growth and fewer flowers.

INTERESTING KINDS: Many cultivars, including reddish 'Clementine', orange-yellow 'Bartley Schwartz', 'Marion Stewart' with orange flowers with red veins. 'Moonchimes' is compact with yellow flowers. Brazilian maple (*A. pictum* 'Thomsonii') has creamy-yellow variegated foliage and pale orange bells with red veins.

Cigar Plant
Cuphea ignea
Sun or light shade

Cute, ever-flowering bunches of small flowers are super attractive to hummingbirds.

FLOWER: Small clusters of tubular flowers, nearly three inches long, that are bright orange red with a white tip all the way around, and a dark ring at the end.

PLANT: Compact plant usually under two feet tall and as wide with narrow, dark green leaves an inch or more long. Used as filler in small flower beds or as a border plant. Pinch tips of new growth to encourage bushier plants with more flowers.

INTERESTING KINDS: 'Lutea' has flowers that are a soft yellow; 'Petite Peach' is peach colored. Relatives include Mexican heather (*C. hyssopifolia*) and "bat face" (*C. llavea*), a re-seeder with red and purple flowers.

Clerodendrum or Glory Bower

Clerodendrum species

Part sun, part shade, shade

Incredibly, this entire group of hardy, dependable, showy, exotic perennials is ignored in most garden books—probably because they are so easy to grow they have become common—and some are fairly invasive to the point of being weedy. But where contained, they are fantastic flowering plants for shade, found in thousands of gardens in all parts of Florida.

FLOWER: Terminal spiky, round, or airy panicles of showy flowers are produced during the entire warm season on new growth. Some are excellent cut flowers. Many produce showy metallic berry-like fruits.

Blue Glory Bower

PLANT: Upright shrubby or spreading plants with large, oval, pointed leaves up to a foot long or wide, sometimes with a disagreeable odor like peanut butter gone bad. Some kinds are extremely invasive, but their excess is easily pulled up to keep colonies in bounds—if you keep at it every spring when new growth arises.

INTERESTING KINDS:

Blue Glory Bower (*C. ugandense*) may not be winter hardy in some northern counties (except with lots of mulch), but can become a small tree covered with airy, blue flowers, each with one violet-blue petal and four pale blue ones and long, arching stamens.

Cashmere Bouquet or **Mexicali Rose** (*C. bungei*) is a very invasive shade plant with large, very dark green leaves topped with mounded flower clusters of rosy pink and light pink. Did I mention that it can become a weed? *C. fragrans* is similar to cashmere bouquet except not as smelly, and with pinkish white double flowers resembling hydrangeas.

Java Glory Bower (*C. speciossima*) has large, hairy, heart-shaped leaves and brilliant scarlet flowers throughout the entire warm season. 'Bornea Sunset' has burgundy leaves and red-orange flowers, and rarely suckers.

Pagoda Flower (*C. paniculatum*) is a very hardy tropical perennial to six feet tall with huge panicles of small orange-red blooms; tolerates quite a bit of sun.

Turk's Turban (*C. indicum*) has very interesting late-summer spikes of white tube-shaped flowers (it is also called "tubeflower") that open just at the ends like frilly knobs.

Pagoda Flower

"INVASIVE" IS A STATE OF MIND. Some of these plants tend to "run" a little, but can be either edged, mowed, or planted where they can do as they please without eating the rest of the garden. Besides, though in college I was taught that a weed is "a plant out of place"— a rose growing in a corn patch, or an oak seedling coming up in the crack of a sidewalk; but I once heard someone say that a better definition of a weed is "any plant having a deal with an unhappy human." Grow what you like, but help it mind its manners.

Coral Bean or Cherokee Bean

Erythrina herbacea

Sun, part sun, part shade

Often considered a shrub, this naturalized native is one of the most drought-hardy plants in Florida—it will rot in irrigated areas of the landscape!

FLOWER: Bright cardinal red, thin, two-inch blooms are produced all around tall spikes continuously from spring to summer, followed by long bean-like seedpods; red seeds are poisonous.

PLANT: Woody, shrub-like plant to three to four feet tall and wide, sends branches up from a woody bulb-like underground base, with widely-spaced leaves of three leaflets. Stems and leaf petioles have sparse, short spines. Cut tall flowering stems back after blooming.

INTERESTING KINDS: Cry-baby (*E. crista-galli*) has a loose, spike-like cluster of short flowers that drip nectar. This plant gets to ten feet or more high.

Coreopsis

Coreopsis species

Sun or light shade

Coreopsis has been widely planted along highways and interstates; usually one or more of the thirteen species that grow wild in Florida (eight are natives) can be seen along back roads.

FLOWER: Daisy-like flowers up to two inches across have many ray flowers with "pinked" or jagged tips, from spring to summer. Most are golden or yellow, but there are burgundy and even pink forms. Some hybrids are double flowering.

PLANT: Not showy, can be clump-forming or rosettes, or tall and airy. Some are creeping perennials with thin leaves. Most are short-lived but reseed prolifically.

INTERESTING KINDS: Tickseed (*C. leavenworthii*) is the official state wildflower, and grows well in all areas. *C. grandiflora* 'Early Sunrise' is widely available from garden centers.

Daylily

Hemerocallis species and hybrids
Full sun to light shade

"Wherever the sun shines, there is a daylily," says Southern perennial guru Allan Armitage. These most eagerly grown perennials are mainstays of the summer flower garden. Find tips on growing and hybridizing daylilies, plus growers near you, through the American Hemerocallis Society (www.daylilies.org).

FLOWER: Large, six-petaled flowers from two to over six inches across, borne on sturdy stems from six inches to six feet tall. Colors range from pale yellow to blackish red, with everything in between except for pure white and pure blue; flowers can be single colors or have contrasting eyes and throats, or be bicolored, banded, tipped, or edged. Flowers are edible, and can be served any way broccoli is used.

PLANT: Many flattened fans of long, slender, grass-like foliage grow from a central crown into clumps one to three feet tall and wide. Rust disease seems to be worse on over-fed, over-watered plants.

INTERESTING KINDS: With over 20,000 named cultivars, there are way too many "best" daylilies to mention here. My two favorites are the nearly wild old orange species (*Hemerocallis fulva*) and 'Stella d'Oro', a foot-high miniature often used as a border or in mass plantings.

THE SINGLE MOST COMMONLY GROWN DAYLILY, the old orange one seen growing along ditches, beside country homes, and in cemeteries—and even found in famous botanical gardens—is despised by "society" daylily growers because of its very commonness. Yet it and the double-flowering variety *kwanso* continue to be popular with new and cottage gardeners alike. They do not cause other daylilies to "revert" to the orange species form, but can spread from runners to crowd out less vigorous daylilies.

Firespike
Odontonema strictum
Sun, part sun, part shade

One of the showiest summer and fall flowering plants, this Central America native is a shrub in South Florida, and will easily survive northern county winters—and butterflies and hummingbirds visit the flowers continuously.

FLOWER: Foot-long spikes of bright red tubular flowers are produced above and contrast starkly against glossy foliage, from midsummer through fall.

PLANT: Massive multi-stemmed shrub with oval, shiny, deep green leaves up to eight to ten inches long that create a dense mound. Leaves blacken at frost, but plants return from roots in all parts of Florida. Can be grown in a large container as well.

INTERESTING KINDS: *O. callistachyum* is taller, with purple flowers that bloom later, and does better in south Florida.

Flags Iris
Iris virginica
Sun, part sun, part shade

Where other irises have a hard time coping with heat, humidity, and lack of cold in the winter, native blue flags do exceptionally well, especially in moist or low areas.

FLOWER: Six-petaled violet blue flowers with three upright "standards" and three "falls" on tall stems in the spring.

PLANT: Creeping rhizomes sprout fans of slender, sword-like leaves to four feet tall, which work well as texture in the garden even when plants are not in bloom. Tolerates wet or boggy soils, and is easy to divide.

INTERESTING KINDS: There are several plants sold as "blue flags," so it's best to buy locally or get "starts" from nearby gardens to ensure hardiness. The tall yellow flags (*I. pseudacorus*) is very invasive and should be avoided in Central and South Florida.

Gaura

Gaura lindheimeri

Sun

A surprisingly tough Gulf Coast native, this airy perennial has nearly constant flower production, and is just as constantly loaded with butterflies. Excellent as filler in sunny, dry flower borders.

FLOWER: Long, gently arching stems to three or four feet tall are studded with pink buds that open into inch-long flowers of pink or white. Cutting seeding stalks off will increase the number of new flowers stalks, and reduce its tendency to reseed everywhere.

PLANT: Clump-forming with many thin branches and thin leaves. Deep taproot increases its drought hardiness. No need to divide, just move seedlings.

INTERESTING KINDS: 'Whirling Butterflies' has white flowers larger than other cultivars. 'Siskiyou Pink' has deep maroon buds that open to rose pink flowers, and leaves mottled with maroon.

Geranium

Pelargonium × *hortorum*

Part sun

Though not true "geraniums" (*Geranium* species), this long-blooming, old-fashioned plant with spicy-scented leaves has been favored for lightly shaded gardens for generations.

FLOWER: Short stalks above foliage are topped with clusters of loose single or double flowers in red, vibrant reddish orange, pink, rose, and violet the entire warm season. Cutting faded stems stimulates more flower production.

PLANT: Almost woody lower stems support succulent flowering stems with many large, kidney-shaped or rounded scalloped leaves that are softly fuzzy and fragrant when crushed or clipped. Foliage of most is dark green with a burgundy or maroon band inside the edge. Allow soil to become completely dry between waterings.

INTERESTING KINDS: Heat-tolerant strains, which are less likely to shut down during high summer, include Orbit, Maverick, Americana, and Eclipse.

Gerbera Daisy

Gerbera jamesonii

Sun, part sun, part shade

Perhaps the most stunning, brilliantly colored, highly variable cut flower in Florida, this tough little plant's worst enemy is too much irrigation.

FLOWER: Daisy-like, up to five inches across with petal-like rays around a central disk; can be single, double, or frilly. Colors range from white to red, orange, coral, pink, yellow, and cream. Outstanding cut flowers on long, stiff stems up to eighteen or more inches tall are produced constantly during warm weather.

PLANT: Like giant dandelions with lobed leaves growing in nearly flat clumps. Requires good drainage (plant them with their crowns slightly above the soil around them). May go dormant in northern counties in the winter.

INTERESTING KINDS: The Wolfpack Strain, developed in North Carolina, is exceptionally durable in both dry and wet seasons.

Goldenrod

Solidago species

Full sun or very light shade

This extremely showy autumn bloomer is unfairly blamed for allergies—of which it is innocent.

FLOWER: Clusters of small, bright golden-yellow flowers, formed atop long, stiff stems, produced in the late summer and fall; pinch tips of flowering stems to make the plant more bushy. Excellent, long-lasting cut flower and wild bird, butterfly, and bee plant.

PLANT: Low-growing rosette with tall, usually non-branching stems with narrow leaves. Some species spread rapidly, others do not.

INTERESTING KINDS: Seaside goldenrod (*S. sempervirens*) does very well in all parts of Florida; sweet goldenrod (*S. odora*) is tall, unbranched, and non-invasive, and has anise-scented leaves; rough-leaf goldenrod (*S. rugosa* 'Fireworks') has arching stems to four feet tall; *S. sphacelata* 'Golden Fleece' and hybrid 'Cloth of Gold' are under two feet tall.

Hibiscus
Hibiscus species
Full sun to very light shade

Texas Star

Hibiscus flowers look unreal, and lend the perfect tropical touch to every garden. With the exception of the popular but frost-sensitive, shrubby Chinese hibiscus (*Hibiscus rosa-sinensis*), most hibiscus are hardy in all parts of Florida.

FLOWER: Huge, four-inch to nearly foot-wide, round, funnel-shaped or flat flowers, single or double, in dazzling white, pink, wine, and red, sometimes with contrasting throats or edges.

PLANT: Many-stemmed, deciduous shrub-like clumps to six feet or more tall, with large palmate or heart-shaped leaves. Leggy plants are easily combined with ornamental grasses, cannas, and other bold plants. Very easy to root from cuttings. Whiteflies and other pests can be troublesome, but can be kept somewhat under control with insecticidal soap sprays.

INTERESTING KINDS:

Confederate Rose Mallow (*H. mutabilis*), which flowers in the fall, has large, soft, medium-green leaves and large, single or double, peony-like flowers that change from pure white in the morning to pink, then red as the day progresses.

Redleaf Hibiscus (*H. acetosella*) is frost sensitive, but very showy with maple-like leaves that vary from dark green to deep purplish red and has maroon flowers late in the season.

Rose Mallow (*H. moscheutos*) has very large, "dinner plate" flowers. New cultivars with huge flowers include 'Moy Grande', 'Lord Baltimore', 'Plum Crazy', and others.

Texas Star or **Swamp Mallow** (*H. coccineus*) is tall and many-stemmed with deeply lobed leaves which look like marijuana, and glossy-red five-petaled flowers.

Confederate Rose Mallow

Indian Blanket or Blanket Flower
Gaillardia pulchella
Sun

This is a native plant that will grow and flower under a rural mailbox, in pure sand with no water whatsoever. Really.

FLOWER: Generally flat, two-inch, daisy-like flower heads with many ray petals of yellow, orange, and red, often with contrasting tips, produced constantly all spring, summer, and fall. Abundant seed production increases the number of plants in the colony from year to year.

PLANT: Spreading mound of long floppy stems one to three feet high with soft, hairy leaves, sometimes short-lived but quickly replaced with seedlings. Can spread into nearby areas.

INTERESTING KINDS: 'Red Plume' and 'Yellow Plume' are double flowered. Hybrids (G. × *grandiflora*) have gray-green foliage and three- to four-inch flowers with much flower color variation that includes orange or maroon bands on petals. Look for compact 'Goblin', yellow-and-red 'Torchlight', and others.

Lion's Ear
Leonotus leonurus
Sun or light shade

A 2004 Florida Plant of the Year selection, this is an unusual but attractive plant much loved by butterflies and hummingbirds.

FLOWER: Bright orange, two-inch tubular trumpets in ball-shaped clusters at every leaf node. Excellent forfresh or dried flower arranging.

PLANT: Clumps two to four feet tall and wide, with some-what leafy spires to six feet tall. Plants tend to get leggy unless they are cut back severely in the late winter. The foliage is grayish and aromatic.

INTERESTING KINDS: 'Harrismith White' has white flowers. The annual lion's ear (L. *nepetifolia*) is gangly, up to six or seven feet tall and half as wide; a fantastic hummingbird plant with spiny flower clusters but tends to reseed to the point of being invasive.

Mexican Heather

Cuphea hyssopifolia

Sun, part sun, part shade

Tidy little plants with good green color and numerous flowers, often used as border plants or in masses, in sun or shade.

FLOWER: Tiny florets in pink, purple, red, or white produced constantly during the warm season in masses in nearly every leaf joint near stem tips; very attractive to hummingbirds and small butterflies.

PLANT: Rounded, dense clump of many slightly stiff stems to two feet tall, with narrow, half-inch or longer dark green leaves. May get frozen back in northern Florida counties, but can be cut back and will return reliably the following spring.

INTERESTING KINDS: 'Itsy Bitsy White' and 'Itsy Bitsy Lilac' are only about eight inches high and twice that wide.

Mexican Mint Marigold

Tagetes lucida

Sun or light shade

French tarragon won't grow well in Florida, but this Mexican native—a true perennial marigold—makes a fine culinary herbal substitute. It is often planted in Hispanic or Mexican cemeteries for its showy yellow flowers that appear around the first of November—when it is used in Day of the Dead festivities.

FLOWER: Buttery yellow flowers, less than half an inch long, are produced in nice clusters in the late fall, often late October.

PLANT: Multiple-stem clump dense with narrow, unbranched stalks two to three feet tall, with many narrow leaves that smell strongly of licorice when crushed.

INTERESTING KINDS: Copper Canyon daisy (*T. lemmonii*) is similar, with bright yellow flowers and foliage strongly scented like mint and lemons.

Mexican Petunia
Ruellia brittoniana
Full sun or light shade

A sterile cultivar makes this invasive plant more attractive as a non-stop butterfly and hummingbird garden plant.

FLOWER: Flaring, petunia-like trumpets of blue, pink, or white, two inches across, on spidery stems. Several dozen flowers per clump open every morning and last through the night, during the entire warm season.

PLANT: Many-stemmed shrubby summer perennial, three feet wide by three or four feet tall (sometimes taller in the shade). Leaves are narrow, dark-green, and opposite one another at knobby nodes. Best suited to perennial borders where there is room to spread or in large containers or beside water gardens. Stem cuttings are fast-rooting in water.

INTERESTING KINDS: 'Purple Showers' is a sterile (non-invasive) variety. 'Chi Chi' has pink flowers but is extremly invasive. 'Katie' is a compact, slow-spreading dwarf form with pink and blue flowers.

Mint
Mentha species
Full sun or light shade

Mint helps the medicine go down, brightens the breath, and masks bad odors near the trash bin. And once started, it can be almost difficult to get rid of.

FLOWER: Small, lavender or pinkish white, salvia-like blossoms on stems above foliage, fragrant and edible.

PLANT: Invasive underground rhizomes sprout masses of round to oblong leaves up to an inch and a half long and half as wide. Upright stems of some species are a foot or more tall. Leaves are aromatic with oils, which makes them extremely fragrant when crushed or after a good rain.

INTERESTING KINDS: The most popular (and readily available) include peppermint, lemon or orange mint (M. × *piperita*), spearmint (M. *spicata*), and apple mint (M. *suaveolens*) with its variegated pineapple mint cultivar.

Obedient Plant or False Dragonhead
Physostegia virginiana
Full sun to part shade

This native plant is almost irresistibly beautiful and loaded with hummingbirds and butterflies, but it simply won't stay put, leading everyone who grows it to comment on how it is not very obedient at all.

FLOWER: Inch-long, tubular flowers produced by the dozens and blooming a few at a time from the bottom of straight spikes up to the top. Flowers are "hinged" so they can be swiveled to point in any direction (hence the plant's name). Excellent cut flower.

PLANT: Spreading mass of individual stems three or more feet tall, with long, pointed, deep-green leaves opposite one another on distinctly square stems.

INTERESTING KINDS: 'Summer Snow', 'Bouquet Rose', and the rose-pink 'Vivid' are easily found; 'Variegata' has pink flowers and white-edged foliage. Compact 'Miss Manners' is less invasive.

Parrot Lily
Alstroemeria psittacina
Shade or light shade

Sometimes grown unwittingly as a spreading groundcover, this odd "passalong" perennial can be enjoyed for either its winter foliage or summer cut flowers—or both.

FLOWER: Sturdy, three-foot stems topped with unusual red-and-green flowers marked with purple blotches, arise from roots separate from leaf stalks in the summer. Long-lasting as cut flowers.

PLANT: Rapidly spreading mounds of light green foliage produced on foot-tall stems from the ground. Leaves emerge in late summer and fall and last until after flowering the following summer. This invasive plant can spread under trees and tall shrubs, and should be contained.

INTERESTING KINDS: 'Variegata' has striking white-edged leaves. There are also several colorful florist cut-flower hybrids, most of which rot in hot, humid, wet summers.

Common Sage

Perennial Salvia
Salvia species
Full sun to light shade

One of the hardest summer colors to find is cool blue—and salvias fit the bill perfectly. All are fantastic butterfly plants, and most make good cut flowers as well. *Salvia leucantha*, *S. guaranitica*, and *S.* × 'Indigo Spires' were named Florida Plant of the Year in 2001.

FLOWER: Generally long, tall spikes of blue, purple, white, or red, two-lipped trumpets either spaced singly above one another or packed densely into one solid spike of color. Most hardy salvias are summer flowering, some only in the short days of spring and fall.

PLANT: Spreading masses of stems bear leaves up to four inches long and sometimes nearly as wide, often very fragrant (sage, the widely used culinary herb, is a hardy salvia). Including the flower stalks, salvias can range from a foot or less tall to over five feet tall and wide. Pinching new growth of taller varieties makes them more compact, as will cutting them back after they begin to fade from the first flush of blooms.

INTERESTING KINDS:

Bog Sage (*S. uliginosa*) is an airy plant to about six feet with narrow, fragrant leaves and spikes of pale-blue and white flowers all summer; tolerates dry soil or wet but can be invasive by underground runners.

Brazilian Sage (*S. guaranitica*) is my favorite for its wide leaves and five-foot stems topped with spikes of deep- or clear-blue flowers that are loaded with hummingbirds; it "moves" around my mulched garden by runners, but is not invasive.

Common Sage (*S. officinalis*) is a somewhat short-lived perennial with highly fragrant leaves and many forms, including variegated.

GREAT BUTTERFLY PERENNIALS: clerodendrum, angelonia, buddleia, firespike, purple coneflower, Mexican heather, lion's ear, spotted horsemint, cardinal flower, lemon balm, vervain, wild ageratum, black-eyed Susan, gaura, phlox, false dragonhead, Mexican petunia, cuphea, salvia, goldenrod, butterfly ginger, milkweed, coreopsis

Forsythia Sage (*S. madrensis*) has yellow orange flowers and thick, four-sided stems up to eight feet tall.

Violet Sage

Indigo Spires Salvia (S. × 'Indigo Spires') is large and sprawling but easily pruned into compact form, with narrow, twisted spikes of closely spaced violet-blue flowers during the entire warm season, and purple calyxes that persist after flowers are shed.

Mexican Bush Sage (*S. leucantha*) is a vigorous, upright shrubby plant with velvety leaves and purple calyxes that persist after flowers shed.

Violet Sage (*S. nemorosa* and the similar *S.* × *superba*) is a spreading plant with narrow, erect flowering stems to nearly three feet tall covered with many violet-blue or purple flowers all summer. Cultivars of a similar hybrid, *S.* × *sylvestris*, include 'East Friesland', 'Rose Queen', 'Blauhügel' ('Blue Hill' or 'Blue Mound'), and 'May Night'.

Mexican Bush Sage

Phlox
Phlox species
Full shade to full sun

Spring wouldn't be right, and neither would summer, without phlox. Among our most eye-catching native perennials, different species are so distinct they almost seem unrelated, yet all are tough and easy to grow.

FLOWER: Five-petaled stars up to one inch across of white, blue, pink, lavender, purple, or red (sometimes with contrasting "eyes"), produced in masses on stems above foliage from late winter through late summer (depending on species). Lightly fragrant, incredibly showy, and great for butterflies.

PLANT: Multiple-stemmed plants that generally die down in the winter. Can be creeping woodland ground-huggers or meadow beauties up to five feet tall, with deep-green leaves that are generally oval or oblong. Powdery mildew is a problem on many kinds, and there isn't a lot to be done about it other than thinning out new growth for better air circulation and avoiding over-watering.

INTERESTING KINDS:

Downy Phlox (*P. pilosa*) is another creeper that stays about a foot or so high, but has sturdy cultivars perfect for container or border edging, including 'Chattahoochee' (hybrid with blue flowers with a wine eye), 'Eco Happy Traveler' (deep pink), and 'Ozarkana' (fragrant, light pink with red eye).

Summer Phlox (*P. paniculata*) is the "tall boy" of midsummer, sprouting sturdy multiple stems up to four or five feet tall, topped with football-sized panicles of garish pink or white, purple, lavender, or red. Cultivars include 'Mt. Fuji' (white), 'Bright Eyes' (pink with rosy centers), and 'Robert Poore' (iridescent purple magenta).

Woodland Phlox (*P. divaricata*), also called wild sweet William and blue phlox, is low-growing (under fifteen inches), spreading, and flowers in late winter.

Downy Phlox

118

Princess Flower

Tibouchina urvilleana

Sun, part sun, part shade

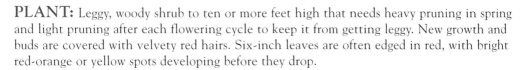

Though woody in South Florida, this Brazilian native is usually cut back nearly to the ground in the winter in north and central areas to keep it from getting too leggy.

FLOWER: Brilliant, showy flowers to three or four inches across with five velvety royal purple petals are produced regularly during the warm season.

PLANT: Leggy, woody shrub to ten or more feet high that needs heavy pruning in spring and light pruning after each flowering cycle to keep it from getting leggy. New growth and buds are covered with velvety red hairs. Six-inch leaves are often edged in red, with bright red-orange or yellow spots developing before they drop.

INTERESTING KINDS: 'Athens Blue' (*T. semidecandra*) has large rich purple flowers with purple stamens and red fall leaves. *T. grandiflora* has huge leaves and flower spikes.

Purple Coneflower

Echinacea purpurea

Full sun to light shade

This native butterfly- and cut-flower perennial is nearly indestructible—unless you pamper it with good soil, fertilizer, and lots of water, which simply cause it to grow too tall and flop over.

FLOWER: Dramatic combination of a thumb-sized, bristly orange central cone (described as shaped like an old beehive), and long, thin, pink, purple, or white ray petals. The "noses" are favorite sources of nutty seeds for goldfinches and other small winter resident birds.

PLANT: Basal rosette of dark-green, pointy-oval leaves with flowering stems up to three or more feet tall in the spring and summer. Plants spread slowly with underground rhizomes, but seed generously.

INTERESTING KINDS: Big bold varieties include 'Magnus', 'Bravado', and rosy-purple 'Bright Star'; white flowering forms include 'White Swan' and 'White Lustre'.

Root Beer Plant
Piper auritum
Sun, part sun, part shade

A heavy rain, or just brushing by this plant, releases its mild root beer fragrance. Though vigorous to a fault (invasive), its large leaves fill a much-needed void in many shade gardens, and a bold tropical touch.

FLOWER: Thin, upright rat-tail like stalks six to ten inches tall appear in spring and summer, but are often hidden in the foliage.

PLANT: Stout, unbranched stems six to ten or more feet high support an umbrella of large, twelve-inch or more wide, heart-shaped leaves of a pale or medium green, soft and fuzzy underneath. The plants spread readily by runners, and should be cut down every winter to keep them from getting too leggy.

INTERESTING KINDS: *Piper nigrum* is the source of green, white, and black pepper.

Rudbeckia or Black-Eyed Susan
Rudbeckia fulgida
Full sun or very light shade

This summer-flowering native is nearly unkillable in hot, dry beds or containers in reflected heat areas.

FLOWER: Typical black-eyed Susan three inches or so across, with a dark chocolate-brown cone surrounded with many stiff yellow ray petals sticking straight out. Each flowering

stem, up to about two feet high, is many-branched. Brown cones are packed with small nutty seeds favored by winter migrant birds.

PLANT: Flat basal rosettes of pointy-oval leaves that are up to four inches long and half that wide with prominent veins. Plants spread by short runners.

INTERESTING KINDS: 'Goldsturm' is a common, compact form. Other perennial rudbeckias include cut-leaf coneflower with deeply lobed leaves (*R. laciniata* 'Hortensia'), double-flowering 'Golden Glow', and more compact 'Goldquelle'.

Scarlet Milkweed or Bloodflower
Asclepias curassavica
Sun

This milkweed—so-named for its milky sap—is anything but a weed! Its butterfly-attracting flowers and foliage appear during the entire warm season, and bring color and height to butterfly gardens.

FLOWER: Small, star-like, vivid-red flowers are produced constantly in dense, showy clusters atop narrow stems, and are followed by fat pods that open to reveal seeds that sail away on silky "parachutes."

PLANT: Upright plant with several stems to three or four feet tall, with narrow leaves up to six inches long. Monarch butterflies lay eggs on the plants for caterpillar food.

INTERESTING KINDS: 'Silky Gold' has yellow-orange flowers. Relatives include butterfly weed (*A. tuberosa*) whose Gay Butterflies strain has red, yellow orange, pink, or bicolored flowers, and tall swamp milkweed (*A. incarnata*) with pink flowers.

Showy Mexican Primrose
Oenothera speciosa
Sun

A very common roadside wildflower, this native can thrive in the heat of a crack in a parking lot curb. Though it will spread vigorously throughout a flower bed in practically no time, when not in bloom it virtually disappears. It is hard to find commercially, but is very durable once it is found and planted.

FLOWER: Fragrant, two-inch-wide single flowers are white but fade to pink and are very showy in spring and early summer.

PLANT: Vigorously-spreading rosettes of green leaves die back after flowering as if they were never there.

INTERESTING KINDS: 'Alba' is pure white, 'Rosea' light pink, 'Siskiyou' is pink, and 'Woodside White' has a pink eye.

Spiderwort
Tradescantia virginiana
Full sun to deep shade

This hard-to-kill native was so important a discovery that it became the namesake of John Tradescant, the most famous English plant explorer. Some weed!

FLOWER: Distinct, three-petaled blue, white, pink, reddish, or purple flowers, up to an inch and a half across, produced in small clusters atop knee-high stems. Flowers open just for one day; direct sunshine closes them.

PLANT: Clump of grass-like arching stems two feet tall. Cutting the plant to the ground only makes it come back stronger.

INTERESTING KINDS: Pure white 'Innocence'; pale lavender with deep blush 'Bilberry Ice'; deep blue 'Zwanenberg; 'Purple Dome'; 'Red Cloud'; 'Purple Profusion' with wine tinted, bluish leaves; and compact 'Sweet Kate' with chartreuse leaves and deep blue flowers.

Spotted Horsemint
Monarda punctata
Sun or light shade

A common native plant in moist areas, this mint relative is a hardy native butterfly plant with clusters of edible flowers that can also spread along dry railroad tracks. It is much tougher in the Florida climate than other *Monarda* species.

FLOWER: Midsummer flowers with showy, whorled clusters of purple-spotted pink or yellow blooms per stem.

PLANT: Bushy, spreading clump to three feet tall with fragrant leaves.

INTERESTING KINDS: Other more showy *Monarda* species that are less tolerant of drought and humidity include bergamot (*M. fistulosa*) and bee balm (*M. didyma*), with mildew-resistant 'Jacob Cline' very commonly seen in woodsy, lightly shaded Florida gardens. Florida horsemint (*Pycnanthemum floridanum*) is a very similar relative, a carefree Florida native with very pungent foliage.

Stokes' Aster
Stokesia laevis
Sun or light shade

Named a Florida Plant of the Year in 2003, this native plant looks like fat monkey grass—until it comes into bloom, when it reveals itself to be one of the best flowering perennials for Florida borders.

FLOWER: Two-foot-tall, many-branched clusters of large, powder-puff buttons that open up to four inches wide from late spring to late summer, mostly blue with some pink, purple, white, and even yellow forms. Stems often flop under the weight of the flowers.

PLANT: Foot-tall clump of smooth, long, grass-like leaves up to six or eight inches long and one inch wide. Easy to divide.

INTERESTING KINDS: Standard varieties include 'Blue Danube', heavy-blooming 'Bluestone', 'Purple Parasols', deep purple 'Wyoming', white 'Silver Moon', and lemon yellow 'Mary Gregory'. 'Color Wheel' has three shades of colors at the same time.

Sunflower
Helianthus species
Full sun

Very dependable tall native flower for fall blooms in the back of a border.

FLOWER: Daisy flowers with many long golden-yellow ray florets, arranged in loose clusters atop tall, many-branched flowering stems.

PLANT: Many-stemmed to over eight feet tall with long, narrow leaves. Needs either staking or pinching in midsummer to prevent flopping under the weight of many autumn flowers.

INTERESTING KINDS: Narrow-leaf or swamp sunflower (*Helianthus angustifolius*) is great in low, wet areas or ordinary garden soils. Jerusalem artichoke (*H. tuberosus*) is a rapidly spreading hedge-forming perennial with large leaves (up to eight inches long) and bright yellow flowers in the fall; its tubers, which are prolific reproducers, are perfectly edible and even sold in grocery stores.

Yarrow
Achillea species
Full sun

This heirloom flowering perennial was introduced by colonists to wrap cuts and wounds.

FLOWER: Small white, yellow, golden, pink, cerise, or red flowers in large, flat clusters up to four or five inches across, atop sturdy stems from two to three or more feet tall.

PLANT: Spreading clump of stems up to a foot or more tall with ferny, fragrant, evergreen, finely divided, soft leaves. Most yarrows spread aggressively, but have trouble coping with excessive rainfall and high humidity if not planted with perfect drainage.

INTERESTING KINDS: Common yarrow (*Achillea millefolium*) has the most fern-like leaves and includes 'Rose Beauty', red 'Paprika' and 'Summer Pastels'. Best cut-flower yarrows (mostly *A. filipendulina*) include 'Coronation Gold'. Hybrids include yellow 'Moonshine', mixed-yellow 'Anthea', and pink 'Appleblossom'.

 Best for Beginners:

- Artemisia
- Banana
- Clerodendrum
- Daylily
- Firespike
- Goldenrod
- Indian Blanket
- Mexican Mint Marigold
- Mint
- Salvia
- Yarrow

Kinda Tricky:

- Coreopsis
- Dayflower
- Gerbera Daisy
- Iris
- Mexican Petunia (invasive)
- Princess Flower
- Spiderwort (invasive)

Other Good Perennials:

Candlestick Plant (*Senna alata* or *Cassia alata*) can be a tree in South Florida or a semi-tender annual in North Florida, but everywhere it's stunning for its big compound leaves and stems topped with large spikes of golden yellow fall flowers.

Cardinal Flower (*Lobelia cardinalis*) is a native perennial for wet areas, with late summer and early fall spikes of cardinal-red flowers that hummingbirds find irresistible. Flowers well in the light shade. 'Queen Victoria' is especially striking with its red leaves.

Dayflower (*Commelina* species) is a lightweight rambling native with sparse flowers that have two sky blue petals. It is impossible to find commercially, but appears on its own in naturalistic gardens and informal borders.

Evening Primrose

Evening Primrose (*Oenothera biennis*) is native in North Florida, and brings the evening garden to life with color and moths. Four- to five-foot spikes of fragrant, clear yellow blossoms yield many seeds, and seedlings that spring up everywhere.

Lemon Balm (*Melissa officinalis*) is a mint relative with large, lemon-scented leaves and dense spires of flowers that attract many species of butterflies and bees.

Shasta Daisy (*Leucanthemum* × *superbum*), a true spring daisy, has pure white ray flowers surrounding a golden central disk, outstanding as a cut flower but somewhat floppy in hot humid climates.

Vervain (*Verbena bonariensis*), a native to South America, has become a naturalized wildflower in Florida, but is perfect as a companion to other perennials, where its tall, loose spikes of brilliant purple flowers contrast with bolder plants. Very good for butterflies, too.

Wild Ageratum or **Mistflower** (*Eupatorium coelestinum*) is a spreading mass of many stems to two feet tall, topped in the late summer and fall with fluffy clusters of powdery blue flowers. Vigorous native spreader that can be difficult to control; outstanding for butterflies and edges of naturalistic or meadow gardens.

Wild Indigo (*Baptisia alba*) is three feet or more tall and wide, with clusters of white pea-like flowers on stiff stems in the late spring and early summer.

Mistflower

Tacky or Gaudy?

As if Hawaiian ti plants, crotons, and bougainvillea vines aren't gaudy enough, gardeners in the Sunshine State seem overly indulgent of kitsch. Not that kitsch is entirely bad. Generally thought of condescendingly as a sign of "low brow" taste, it can also represent a sense of irony ("this stuff is so bad, it's good"). More than simply art gone wrong, it allows ordinary people to participate in romantic fantasy, or poke fun at the sometimes bittersweet blandness of life.

Besides, there is a tacit difference between "gaudy" and "tacky." Gaudy is when you do something that others may not like, but they cut you some slack if they think you know what you're doing. Tacky, on the other hand, is when you just don't know any better—bless your heart! But filmmaker John Waters even defined the difference between good and bad tacky: "Good tacky looks up to its subject; bad tacky looks down."

Take plastic pink flamingos—America's most loved-to-be-hated icon, patented in 1957 by Massachusetts art school graduate Donald Featherstone. His company churns out over 250,000 pairs of flamingos a year—and not all go into the yards of the terminally tacky. "I don't think it's always a joke," Featherstone said. "The majority of the people who buy them just really feel that

an empty yard, like an empty coffee table, cries out for something. They don't do it for themselves, but to entertain you.

"We actually sell more plastic ducks than flamingos, but I gotta say, the duck people aren't like flamingo people. Folks who put out flamingos are friendlier than others."

So if you have a hankering to add to your yard a giant seashell, old boat, mini-lighthouse, concrete seahorse, cutout mermaids, nylon hibiscus flag, fake pirate cannon, seahorse party lights, or a cute mailbox made to look like a manatee, alligator, dolphin, mermaid, sea turtle, fish, pelican, or surfboard, keep in mind what Featherstone once told me: "Before plastic, only the wealthy could afford to have poor taste."

STEADFAST
Shrubs

Want to really have a low-maintenance landscape that looks good every month of the year? Your choice of shrubs, and how they are planted that very first time, can make or break the landscape.

Along with trees, vines, and palms, long-lived woody shrubs create the basic framework around which other flowers revolve. They are the "bones" of the garden, providing year-round focal points, lines, hedges, masses, and security. Plus, when compared with annuals and perennials, and especially the lawn, shrubs are generally very low maintenance. This chapter is packed with over four dozen of the best ones, each recommended by some of Florida's top garden experts as being beautiful, useful, tough enough for the sandy soils and climate, and creating a "sense of place" unique to any other spot on Earth. There are many other good shrub choices, but the ones here keep rising to the top of the heap for durability and beauty—including some that many garden designers once turned away from as "old-fashioned" or common.

Not-So-Secret Secrets for Success

Getting shrubs in place and able to thrive over the long haul is easy, if you follow these simple tips: Choose good plants, place them in appropriate conditions (sun or shade, wet soil or dry), dig a wide hole, and loosen the roots when planting. Adding soil amendments means just that—adding to, not replacing, your native soil. Mulches, deep soakings, and light feedings can

help get plants established so well they can survive— even thrive—for decades with little or no attention. Really. Oh, and if your underlying soil is mucky or clay, dig a little deeper and raise the bed up a little higher, so plants don't stay too wet during rainy spells, or too dry during lean times.

Best for Beginners:

- *Abelia*
- *Althea*
- *Century Plant*

- *Cleyera*
- *Hollies*
- *Ligustrum*

- *Loropetalum*
- *Oleander*
- *Prickly Pear*

- *Shrub Roses*
- *Soft-Tip
  Yucca*

Kinda Tricky:

- *Azaleas*
- *Boxwood* (nematodes)

- *Camellia*
- *Elaeagnus*

- *Red-Tip Photinia*
- *Yellow Bells*

Year-Round Texture Is Easy

Keeping in mind the ideal textural combination of "spiky, roundy, and frilly," you can have an interesting twelve-month landscape by combining several kinds of shrubs with contrasting forms and foliage. My favorites include the bright green, teardrop-shaped arborvitae contrasted perfectly with the burgundy winter foliage of heavenly bamboo (nandina); throw in a soft-tip yucca, and an airy, tree-form yaupon holly, and you'll have an eye-catching combo! Even crape myrtles, sumac, or althea look better when underplanted with groundcover junipers, dwarf yaupon, or dwarf nandina. Mix and match at a garden center to see what works for you.

Birds Love Shrubs

Not only do shrubs provide texture, flowers, and fragrance for our garden, they also make terrific perching, feeding, and nesting sites for native birds. Anything evergreen or with berries is a plus, but the real key to providing good wildlife habitat is diversity—special attention needs to be given to planting something for all seasons, because, after all, our native wildlife is out there all year, not just in the seasons convenient for humans.

Shrubs with good bird fruits include holly, Simpson's stopper, beautyberry, elaeagnus, ligustrum, prickly pear cactus, and sumac. Examples of good shrubs that provide good cover include abelia, arborvitae, camellia, cleyera, elaeagnus, hollies, and ligustrum. There are many others, of course.

Abelia

Abelia × grandiflora

Sun or shade

This long-blooming favorite for humming-birds, butterflies, and moths can be sheared tightly or allowed to ramble informally.

FLOWER: Clusters of small white to pink tubular bells, spring through fall, surrounded with pink sepals that persist after the flowers fall off, almost like small pink blossoms.

PLANT: Evergreen shrub, three to six feet tall and wide, with graceful arching branches covered with small, glossy, pointed, oval leaves of green with a bronze cast in the fall.

INTERESTING KINDS: 'Francis Mason' is compact and dense with pink flowers and variegated leaves; 'Golden Glow' has yellow foliage; 'Prostrata' makes a dependable groundcover for slopes. 'Edward Goucher' is dwarf, airy, and pink-flowering. Chinese abelia (*A. chinensis*) has large, thick clusters of flowers.

Arborvitae

Thuja occidentalis

Full sun to part shade

The "tree of life" is an old standby tough enough for cemetery conditions. Its brilliant green color and dependable shape make it indispensable for garden "oomph."

FLOWER: No obvious flowers, just interesting small, bumpy, round blue cones in winter.

PLANT: Teardrop, round, or irregularly shaped shrubs of dense emerald or golden frond-like fans of tiny scale-like leaves.

INTERESTING KINDS: 'Emerald' is a dense, narrow cone to about fifteen feet tall and four feet wide; 'Globosa' remains tightly rounded to about three feet ('Little Gem' and 'Little Giant' are similar); 'Rheingold' is cone-shaped, slow-growing, and bright golden, only four or five feet tall; 'Woodwardii' is an old-fashioned globular arborvitae that grows very slowly to about eight feet. 'Degroot's Spire' and 'Brabant' are narrow and columnar.

Aucuba
Aucuba japonica
Shade

This large evergreen shade shrub, which is most dependable in North Florida, tolerates deep shade, and even competes well with tree roots. Variegated forms can brighten dark corners in the shaded garden.

FLOWER: Inconspicuous maroon flowers hidden in the foliage, followed by clusters of large, bright red berries on female plants (male plants are needed nearby for fruit).

PLANT: Medium to large evergreen for dense shade with large oval pointed leaves that are a dark polished green but often spotted with yellow. It will burn in the sun, even in mid-winter under deciduous trees.

INTERESTING KINDS: 'Variegata', the "gold dust plant," has many yellow spots on each green leaf; 'Picturata' has one large gold spot; 'Sulphur' has a gold edge; 'Rozanne' is self-fruitful.

Beautyberry
Callicarpa americana
Moderate shade to full sun

A native of Southern woodlands, this "French mulberry" or "Spanish mulberry" is a real show-stopper with gaudy berries prized by birds.

FLOWER: Three-inch clusters of small, pinkish flowers appear on either side of leaf joints from late spring to midsummer, followed by tight, golf-ball-sized clusters of small bright magenta-purple berries.

PLANT: Rounded shrub to six feet tall and nearly as wide with long, arching branches covered loosely with hand-sized oval, light-green leaves. Heavy winter pruning will keep leggy plants in bounds.

INTERESTING KINDS: 'Lactea' has white berries. Chinese beautyberry (*C. dichotoma*) has finer textured leaves and slender branches that sweep to the ground, with violet berries. Japanese beautyberry (*C. japonica*) gets up to five feet tall and wide with good fall leaf colors of orange and reddish purple.

Camellia

Camellia japonica
and Camellia sasanqua
Part shade to sun

Many gardeners are surprised to learn that "all the tea in China" is made from the leaves of the little-grown *Camellia sinensis*, a large evergreen shrub with small white flowers in the late summer and early fall. The two most popular camellias—*C. sasanqua* and *C. japonica*—flower from fall to spring, sun or shade, which is why they are often called the "rose of winter."

FLOWER: Large, showy, open "roses" up to five or more inches across produced in the fall (*C. sasanqua*) and winter (*C. japonica*), either single or double red, white, pink, blotched, or striped—with over three thousand different cultivars from which to choose.

PLANT: Tall, rounded evergreen to ten or more feet tall, with pointed, shiny, oval leaves up to five inches long. Plants require an acidic soil high in organic matter, and lots of mulch.

INTERESTING KINDS: Popular old "japonicas" include 'Pink Perfection', 'Professor Sargeant', 'Debutante', and 'Betty Sheffield'; "sasanquas" include red 'Yuletide', white 'Mine-No-Yuki', and rich, ruby red peony form 'Sparkling Burgundy'. 'Shishi-Gashira' (*Camellia × hiemalis*) is a rose-red semi-double that blooms from fall to spring, and was named a Florida Plant of the Year in 2004.

CAMELLIAS, LIKE AZALEAS, LOVE ACIDIC SOILS. Work peat moss into your soil at planting time, and use an acid-forming azalea-camellia specialty fertilizer around established shrubs.

Century Plant

Agave americana

Full sun or part shade

The word "wicked" comes up in conversations about this incredibly bold accent plant. Though each plant dies after flowering, it quickly grows many smaller plants at the base, called "pups." Still, it is an excellent speciment for dry or beach-type conditions.

FLOWER: Tall, tree-like stem up to thirty or even forty feet tall topped with branches of yellow-green flowers, appearing usually on plants ten years or more old. Very attractive to hummingbirds.

PLANT: Monstrous clump of blue-green or variegated leaves, three to six feet long, thick at the base but narrowing to a stiff spine, with hooked spines along the leaf edges. Must have excellent drainage.

INTERESTING KINDS: There are variegated kinds with broad yellow or white stripes on each leaf, and several smaller or more compact species, some with bluish leaves and reddish flowers.

Chinese Fringe

Loropetalum chinense

Sun or part sun

New varieties of this very low maintenance shrub bring fiery red foliage and deep pink flowers to gardens.

FLOWER: Clusters of creamy white, pink, or nearly fuchsia flowers, each with four narrow, twisted petals, bloom in late winter and spring, some continuing to fall.

PLANT: Small to medium shrub, fast growing to five to fifteen feet, depending on the cultivar, with compact but numerous tiers of arching or drooping branches, and rounded leaves that can be green or burgundy.

INTERESTING KINDS: 'Burgundy' has red new growth fading to green; 'Suzanne' is compact with rounded, reddish maroon leaves; 'Fire Dance' and 'Pipa's Red' hold deep red foliage color all summer. The very popular 'Ruby' can be easily kept to three to four feet high with regular pruning.

Copper Plant or Copperleaf
Acalypha wilkesiana
Sun or light shade

Bulky mainstay foliage plant for accent, specimen, or summer hedge. Will probably freeze in North Florida but makes a very hardy woody shrub in Central and South Florida. Incredibly heat and drought tolerant.

FLOWER: Not very showy tassels of reddish brown hanging from leaf axils.

PLANT: Three-foot or taller mass of mottled bronze, red, copper, orange, and green foliage, held densely around the plant. A great "anchor" for companions in a large container, in groups, or as a short backdrop to other flowers.

INTERESTING KINDS: 'Macafeeana' has large reddish leaves tinged with crimson and bronze; 'Hoffmannia' has narrow, twisted leaves; 'Obovata' has leaves ruffled and serrated, in pink, bronze, and red.

Elaeagnus
Elaeagnus pungens
Sun or shade

Have a school bus you want to hide? Not much would beat elaeagnus. And if you like to prune, this is the shrub for you!

FLOWER: Half-inch white tubes in fall, sweetly fragrant, are followed by winter fruits that are prized by birds.

PLANT: Mounding, naturalistic evergreen to fifteen feet high and wide, with long, willowy, moderately thorny stems and leaves mottled green above, silvery beneath.

INTERESTING KINDS: Showy variegated cultivars include 'Maculata' with golden yellow centers; 'Aurea' and 'Variegata' with gold edges to green leaves; 'Sunset' has bright-yellow foliage. 'Ebbingei' is a very popular compact form. The legendary "gumi" (or "goumi") bush (*E. multiflora*), including several forms such as 'Crispa' and variety *ovata*, is smaller, flowers in the spring, and has attractive scarlet, edible fruit an inch in diameter.

Fatsia

Fatsia japonica

Shade or part sun

Talk about bold—this coarse-textured shrub makes a strong statement in heavy shade, with long stalk-like stems topped with tropical foliage. It also works as a potted indoor plant.

FLOWER: Short spikes above the foliage of rounded clusters of small, creamy white flowers in fall and early winter, sometimes followed by clusters of small, shiny, black berries.

PLANT: Upright, spreading, colony-forming evergreen to five to eight feet tall and wide, with large deeply lobed, fanlike leaves up to nearly eighteen inches wide. Spreads slowly but surely by suckers into a dense mass.

INTERESTING KINDS: 'Variegata' has deep green leaves edged with creamy yellow or golden yellow. 'Moseri' is more compact than the species.

Firebush

Hamelia patens

Shade, part shade, part sun

One of Florida's earliest Plant of the Year selections in 1998, this dependable native, sometimes called "firecracker" shrub for its flower shape, is hardy in all parts of the state, though a hard winter turns it into a herbaceous perennial in northern counties.

FLOWER: Clusters of bright reddish orange tubular flowers are produced at the tips of stems all summer, and are nearly constant attractants for hummingbirds and butterflies.

PLANT: Gardenia relative to eight or ten feet tall or more and half as wide, with whorls of six-inch long oval leaves that are gray-green, on red stalks. Very tolerant of alkaline or limy soils

INTERESTING KINDS: 'Miami Supreme' has leaves that are red most of the season. 'Compacta' is, well, compact.

Florida Anise
Illicium floridanum
Shade or part shade

This Florida woodland native makes a dense hedge or screen for shade, and has interesting flowers and scented foliage.

FLOWER: Golf-ball-size red or white spring flowers with many narrow petals are in leaf axils and sometimes hidden in foliage.

PLANT: Large evergreen shrub to fifteen feet tall with thick, glossy, oval, pointed leaves that have a distinct anise spicy fragrance when bruised or crushed. Grows best in damp shade but tolerates sun.

INTERESTING KINDS: 'Halley's Comet' is compact and has larger red flowers into fall; 'Woodland Ruby' has ruby pink flowers. Yellow anise (*I. parviflorum*) has yellow flowers, forms small colonies by suckers, and tolerates more sun and drought than Florida anise.

Florida Jasmine
Jasminum floridum
Sun or part sun

A "semi-vining" shrub, this plant makes a huge statement with its contrasting foliage and flowers, and almost cascading form, especially in masses, on slopes, or falling over retaining walls.

FLOWER: Clear yellow trumpets, non-scented, form in clusters at leaf joints; blooms heavily in spring and lightly into fall.

PLANT: Bright green arching branches with three (sometimes five) leaflets per leaf. Can be tied to make a vine-like effect, or pruned to force many smaller branches for a more compact plant.

INTERESTING KINDS: Winter jasmine (*J. nudiflorum*) roots where it touches the ground, but flowers only in the spring. Italian jasmine (*J. humile*) has more erect, willowy shoots to over ten feet tall with fragrant yellow flowers all summer; 'Revolutum' has larger flowers. The sprawling primrose jasmine (*J. mesnyi*) is commonly planted along highway embankments.

Gardenia

Gardenia augusta (G. jasminoides)

Sun, part sun, part shade

Florida's humid summer air is heavy with the sweetly heady fragrance of gardenia, sometimes called cape jasmine.

FLOWER: Intensely fragrant, white, usually double blossoms appear in mid-spring into fall. Faded flowers are a dull, limp yellow.

PLANT: Small to medium size shrub, two to six or more feet, have very glossy leaves that are often covered with black "sooty mold" growing on whitefly and aphid drippings, but can be rinsed off. Leaves turn bright orange yellow before falling a few at a time.

INTERESTING KINDS: 'Mystery' is a large shrub with five- to six-inch flowers; 'Radicans' is a very compact, low-growing plant to only a foot or so tall but spreading. 'August Beauty' is popular for late summer, and 'Veitchii' may bloom even in the winter.

Gold Jasmine

Cestrum aurantiacum

Shade or part shade

A Florida Plant of the Year selection in 2000, this hardy tropical plant is fast growing and sure to please every hummingbird in your neighborhood.

FLOWER: Ends of branches are weighed down with clusters of tubular orange-yellow flowers all summer, followed by white berries that birds love to eat.

PLANT: Woody shrub that often gets killed to the ground in North Florida, but quickly re-grows to ten feet or more, with airy, often arching branches covered with deep green, four-inch leaves. Tip-prune to maintain compactness.

INTERESTING KINDS: The more common red cestrum (*C. elegans*) has purplish red flowers and red berries; Chilean or willow-leaf cestrum (*C. parqui*) and night-blooming jasmine (*C. nocturnum*) are intensely fragrant, with the latter being nearly unbearable for some people.

Holly
Ilex species
Full sun to dense shade

Chinese Holly

Hollies provide the evergreen "bones" of foundation designs, hedges, specimens, and accents around which all the other plants flow through the seasons. Tough and versatile, they come in an astounding range of species, types within each species, and cultivars within each type. Some types are deciduous.

FLOWER: Tight, inch-wide clusters of small, yellowish white flowers appear first thing in the spring on the ends of the previous year's growth. Most hollies have separate male and female plants—you need some of each for berries, which can be drab and black, or showy red.

PLANT: Depending on type, either mounding, upright, or tree-form, usually evergreen with leaves ranging from boxwood-like to three or more inches long, with or without sharp spines, in a range of shades from dusty gray-green to lustrous forest green to dark blue-green.

INTERESTING KINDS: Native hollies include several tree-like types such as American (*I. opaca*), yaupon (*I. vomitoria*), dahoon (*I. cassine*), and possum haw (*I. decidua*). Other great groups of hollies are shrubby Chinese (*I. cornuta*) and Japanese (*I. crenata*), and the more tree-like lusterleaf (*I. latifolia*). There are many very popular hybrids between species.

Japanese Holly

Felder's Holly Picks:

These represent only the most "mainstream" hollies, but they are usually easily found and very dependable:

American: Big woodland trees with very spiny leaves; over three hundred cultivars; favorites include 'Howard' and yellow-fruited 'Callaway'.

Dahoon: Great small understory tree for between pines, with heavy, long-lasting berry set on females and yellow-green leaves (normal for the species).

Chinese: Popular foundation and "parking lot" shrubs with dense, durable, glossy bright-green leaves with or without spines or scarlet red berries; easy to prune into low to medium hedges or to train as tree-form. Cultivars include 'Burfordii', a stout large evergreen with a single spine (even the smaller-leaved dwarf Burford can become large over time); 'Rotunda', dense low mound with very spiny leaves well suited for burglar-proofing or foot traffic control; and 'Carissa', a low-growing single-spine 'Rotunda' variation.

Yaupon: Multi-branched airy native evergreen with gray stems and loose berries, perfect as a specimen or "baffle" (airy almost see-through hedge); 'Pendula' is a striking weeping form, named a Florida Plant of the Year for 2005; 'Will Fleming', a narrow, needle-like, fruitless accent to fifteen feet or more; 'Nana' and 'Schellings Dwarf' are compact round evergreens grown as foundation and other hedge-type shrubs, usually sheared into small gumdrops.

Yaupon Holly

Hybrids: 'Nellie R. Stevens', a popular hybrid, is a very prolific berry producer with deep-green foliage; 'Foster', well-known loose Christmas tree shape with long, dark-green leaves and bright clusters of berries, used as a specimen or large container plant; 'East Palatka', yellow-green small tree with few spines per leaf; 'Savannah', upright small tree with several spines per leaf but great berries.

EXTENSION HORTICULTURIST SYDNEY PARK BROWN of Tampa notes that even the toughest shrubs have to be helped through their first summer, to get estabished. This does not mean using lots of organic backfill, but use lots of mulch—and especially, frequent, deep soakings. Very important!

Indian Hawthorn
Rhaphiolepis species
Sun or part sun

This virtually indestructible shrub is ideal for hot, sunny, dry spots, including parking areas and near the beach. Disease-resistant varieties are edging out older kinds.

FLOWER: Dense spikes of small pale pink, reddish, or white blooms in spring and early summer, followed by dark blue fruits.

PLANT: Evergreen shrub with glossy, leathery leaves that start out tinged with bronze or red. Some varieties can be trained into a small tree-form or pinched to keep them bushy. Leaf-spot diseases can be serious as a result of over-irrigation, too much shade, or heavy rains, but heavy pruning after flowering can remove much of the diseased foliage and stimulate new growth.

INTERESTING KINDS: Leafspot-resistant strains include 'Indian Princess', 'Snow White', 'Olivia', and 'Snow Pink'. Avoid 'Enchantress' and 'Fascination' if possible. 'Majestic Beauty' is a hybrid that becomes very large.

Japanese Cleyera
Cleyera japonica
Full sun to moderate shade

A super-sturdy evergreen shrub grown tree-form or kept clipped in a dense hedge or foundation plant.

FLOWER: Clusters of creamy white, half-inch, very fragrant blossoms appear in late spring. Berries are favored by birds, but can be messy if planted near a deck.

PLANT: Fast-growing, easily pruned evergreen shrub that can grow up to fifteen or more feet tall if unpruned. Thumb-sized leaves appear in whorls at the ends of twigs, and have an almost rubbery feeling, dark on top and light green beneath, with reddish leaf stems. New growth is usually shiny copper-bronze. Easy to prune into small evergreen trees.

INTERESTING KINDS: 'Tricolor' has yellow-and-rose variegation. Cleyera is sometimes referred to in landscape manuals as *Ternstroemia gymnanthera*.

Junipers

Juniperus species

Full sun to light shade

Pfitzer Juniper

Evergreen junipers are as versatile and important as hollies for their wide variety of shapes and landscape uses.

FLOWER: Insignificant, but some species have attractive cones or light blue "berries" in the winter (used to flavor gin).

PLANT: Evergreen with tiny needle-like foliage, sometimes stiff and prickly, sometimes soft. Some forms are informal shrubs, others are upright trees. Junipers cannot be pruned hard, just lightly sheared.

INTERESTING KINDS: Pfitzer (*J.* × *pfitzeriana*, to six feet and spreading, some varieties have golden or silver-blue new growth), Hollywood (*J. chinensis* 'Torulosa', striking upright shrub to twenty feet with thick, irregular growth), Gold Coast (*J. chinensis* 'Gold Coast', three feet by five feet with lacy, yellow foliage), blue point (*J. chinensis* 'Blue Point', a narrow, upright specimen to about eight feet tall), skyrocket (*J. scopulorum* 'Skyrocket', a very narrow, tall spike to fifteen feet tall but only two feet wide). Eastern red cedar (*J. virginiana*) is the most durable evergreen tree ever, with several smaller forms.

Chinese Juniper

Eastern Red Cedar

Ligustrum

Ligustrum species

Sun or shade

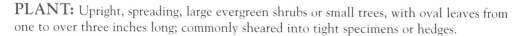

Want a fast evergreen screen, cheap? Then choose ligustrum, also called privet. Plant it well, then run for your clippers.

FLOWER: Small, showy, very fragrant white flower clusters in mid-spring on unpruned shrubs; late summer black fruits are attractive to birds.

PLANT: Upright, spreading, large evergreen shrubs or small trees, with oval leaves from one to over three inches long; commonly sheared into tight specimens or hedges.

INTERESTING KINDS: Japanese ligustrum (*L. japonicum*) is a popular, fast-growing evergreen shrub for foundations, hedges and specimens. The common Chinese privet (*L. sinense*) is too invasive, even the variegated form which often reverts to green. For interest, try *L. texanum* 'Jack Frost' with cream and silvery green leaves.

Nandina

Nandina domestica

Full sun to dense shade

"Heavenly bamboo" is a perfect "textury" contrast with nearly every other plant.

FLOWER: Billowy clusters of small white flowers in mid-spring; pea-sized red berries on old varieties (not recommended where it may become invasive).

PLANT: Slow-spreading clump of slender stalks topped with stiff, ferny foliage. Prune by thinning older canes nearly to the ground.

INTERESTING KINDS: Two berry-less kinds are 'Firepower', a gnarly, twisted, red-and-burnt-orange compact form well suited for hot dry spots or mass planting, and 'Gulf Stream', a dense, dark-green mound with good red foliage in the winter. 'Harbor Dwarf' looks like "regular" nandina, but gets only two to three feet tall and spreads well; 'Compacta' gets to five feet tall and has good berry production in northern counties.

Oleander
Nerium oleander
Sun or part sun

This Florida mainstay is bulky and bold, but unbeatable for spring, summer, and fall flowers, and tolerant of every possible kind of soil or site, from clay to sand, swamp to beach. Note that all parts of the plant are deadly poisonous if eaten; even its stems can impart toxins if used as á skewer when roasting hot dogs.

FLOWER: Very showy clusters of single or double flowers in white, pink, red, or salmon appear on stem tips during the entire warm season.

PLANT: Many stemmed shrub to ten or more feet tall and wide (depending on selection), is dense enough to make a windbreak, with every stem covered with long, narrow leaves up to nearly a foot long.

INTERESTING KINDS: Many cultivars, ranging from four-foot dwarfs such as 'Petite Pink' and 'Dwarf Salmon' to the larger dark pink 'Calypso'.

Pittosporum
Pittosporum tobira
Sun, part sun, part shade

One of the most generic shrubs of all can be pruned into tight balls, limbed up into a tree, or used as a windbreak, specimen, or foundation plant.

FLOWER: Creamy white flowers smell like orange blossoms in the spring, and are followed by not very showy, pea-size fruits.

PLANT: Dense, medium to large shrub can get nearly fifteen feet tall and wide, but can be pruned into a small understory or shade tree. Leaves are oblong, three to five inches long, and grow in whorls at the ends of twigs.

INTERESTING KINDS: 'Wheeler's Dwarf' grows three to five feet high and wide; 'Variegatum' has gray-green leaves edged in white; 'Cream de Mint' is usually less than three feet tall, with bright green leaves edged in white.

143

Plumbago
Plumbago auriculata
Sun, part sun, part shade

Herbaceous in northern counties away from the coast, this airy plant, with welcome cool blue or white summer flowers is widely used as a border, understory, or container plant. Also called cape plumbago.

FLOWER: Very showy clusters of inch-wide flowers of white or blue, with much seedling variation.

PLANT: Mounding shrub five to six feet tall and even wider, with medium-green, oblong leaves that are damaged by frost. Shrub can be pruned hard to keep it in bounds, or tied and trained as a semi-vine.

INTERESTING KINDS: 'Royal Cape' and 'Imperial Blue' are cutting-grown cultivars with predictably good blue color; 'Alba' and 'White Cape' are dependable white forms. Chinese and Burma plumbagos (*Ceratostigma* species) are similar but smaller.

Pomegranate
Punica granatum
Sun, part sun, part shade

One of the most exotic Mediterranean fruits is produced on this large shrub with showy summer flowers. Some varieties are grown for their flowers only.

FLOWER: Large ruffled single or double orange-red flowers in spring and summer are followed by large round leathery balls packed with tart, juicy fruits that can be eaten seed and all.

PLANT: Dwarf to over ten-foot-tall shrubs with pointy oval leaves can be tip-pruned to keep in bounds.

INTERESTING KINDS: Best fruiting varieties include 'Wonderful', 'Sweet', 'Eversweet', and 'Granada'. Flowering-only varieties include 'California Sunset' with white flowers striped with red, dwarf 'Nana' (may produce fruit), and 'Nochi Shibari' with double, dark red flowers.

Prickly Pear Cactus

Opuntia compressa

Full sun to moderate shade

You don't have to be a sadist to enjoy this native cactus, which never needs any care at all. It is very common, and provides a strong "sense of place" in Florida gardens. Combines well with yucca or agave.

FLOWER: Many-petaled tulip-like tufts to four inches across, yellow or orange, in late spring and summer, followed by purplish plum-like edible fruits.

PLANT: Thickened pads, round like pancakes or sometimes elongated, produced on tops of previous growth in an ever-increasing mound. Can be eaten (called *nopales*) by slicing and cooking like green beans.

INTERESTING KINDS: Texas prickly pear (*Opuntia lindheimeri*) is a large, clumping cactus with long pads; *O. drummondii* has very small pads, under three inches across and very thorny; my favorite is the thornless form.

Red Tip Photinia

Photinia fraseri

Sun, part sun, part shade

This occasionally overplanted large shrub is a popular and showy "red hedge" plant, very dependable when not planted too close together, which creates disease conditions.

FLOWER: Showy flat clusters of white flowers in the spring followed by orange-red berries.

PLANT: Upright, dense shrub to fifteen feet tall, can be kept sheared smaller. New growth is bright red, very attractive against older green leaves. Defoliating leafspot diseases are serious where shrubs are planted too close together (less than six feet apart) or irrigated too often.

INTERESTING KINDS: 'Red Robin' is compact and has disease resistance. Japanese photinia (*P. glabra*) has better berries and coppery-red new growth. Chinese photinia (*P. serrulata*) is a huge evergreen with stunning large flower and fruit clusters and distinctly bronze new growth.

Rose

Rosa species and hybrids

Full sun to very light shade

For too long, high-maintenance rose hybrids have dominated the market place, when there are quite a few very attractive, nearly pest-free varieties and species that show up in old or country gardens that are truly easy to grow.

FLOWER: Colorful pointed buds borne either singly on long stems or in loose masses. Buds open into many petals of red, white, pink, yellow, orange, burgundy, and near blue; single or double, some open flowers remain tight while others flop open shamelessly. Many are heady with fragrant perfume. Though some old varieties bloom only once in the spring, most continue to flower off and on through the summer and right up to the first frost of autumn. Pruning stimulates increased new flowering shoot and bud formation, but many flower repeatedly with no pruning at all.

PLANT: Small compact bushes to tall leggy shrubs and a few multiple-stemmed vines. Most are thorny. Foliage of many hybrids is susceptible to diseases (black spot and powdery mildew) for which even regular fungicide sprays have only moderate success at best, but many good ones are fairly disease-free.

INTERESTING KINDS: In general, there are five main kinds of roses most popular in Florida: hybrid tea (upright with long stems and pointed buds, most susceptible to diseases); polyantha (small to medium bushes with solid masses of small flowers); floribunda (larger bushes with masses of larger flower clusters); old garden roses (shrubby and climbing roses that have been around since before the 1860s); and species roses (not hybrids, have been around forever). There are others, of course.

'The Fairy'

Felder's Picks: A Dozen Roses That Won't Break Your Heart

- **'Bonica'** (pink shrub)

- **Butterfly Rose,** *Rosa chinensis mutabilis* (large mixed-color shrub)

- **'Carefree Delight'** (sturdy pink shrub)

- **'Duchesse de Brabant'** (fragrant old garden shrub)

- **'Europeana'** (red floribunda)

Butterfly Rose

'La Marne'

- **'First Edition'** (pink floribunda)

- **'Knockout'** (ever-blooming red)

- **'La Marne'** (pink compact polyantha)

- **'Louis Philippe'** (mauve shrub)

- **'Mister Lincoln'** (red hybrid tea)

- **'Old Blush'** (pink old garden shrub)

- **'The Fairy'** (light-pink small polyantha)

ROSE EXPERTS SAY YOU SHOULD PRUNE ROSES right above an outward-facing five-leaflet leaf. Truth is, you can prune them with firecrackers, and they'll still bloom. The main thing to remember for pruning shrub roses is whack them low in the late winter for size control, then shear or thin as needed through the summer.

Rosemary
Rosmarinus officinalis
Sun or part sun

One of the most popular Mediterranean herbs for warm climates, this upright or cascading shrub brightens every garden with its form and fragrance, especially after a rain releases its essential oils.

FLOWER: Small, blue or lavender-blue edible flowers are clustered in leaf axils from fall to spring.

PLANT: Many upright or cascading stems are stiff, and covered with typically thin one-inch or longer leaves that are dark green above and grayish green underneath. Leaves are very aromatic, with culinary value.

INTERESTING KINDS: 'Blue Spires' is vigorous and upright to five feet tall and wide, with deep blue flowers; can be sheared into a hedge. 'Prostratus' hangs almost straight down when planted above a retaining wall or in a large pot. There are many others.

Simpson's Stopper
Myrcianthes fragrans
Sun or part sun

Also called twinberry, this Florida native was named a Plant of the Year in 2002 for its general toughness and many uses. "Stopper" allegedly comes from the berries being used to treat diarrhea.

FLOWER: Small white, frilly, fragrant flowers are produced in the spring, followed by reddish-orange berries that attract birds.

PLANT: Evergreen shrub, five to ten feet tall with cinnamon colored bark, has small glossy leave. Easy to shear for more density, though this reduces flowering.

INTERESTING KINDS: 'Compacta' has coppery red new growth. Other "stoppers" in the *Eugenia* genus are hardy in South and south Central Florida, and include the invasive Surinam cherry (*E. uniflora*) with showy white flowers and edible summer fruits. 'Lolita' has delicious sweet black fruits for jelly making.

Tea Olive
Osmanthus fragrans
Sun, part sun, part shade

The old Southern favorite "tea olive" is big and powerful—in size and fragrance, at a time of year when it is most welcome. Often planted with camellias, which are prettier in flower but have little or no fragrance of their own.

FLOWER: Small clusters of extremely fragrant white flowers in leaf axils in spring, fall, and winter.

PLANT: Dense evergreen to fifteen feet tall can reach twenty-five or more feet with age. Glossy oval leaves are edged or toothed. Plants grow best with light shade, especially in the hot afternoon.

INTERESTING KINDS: *Osmanthus fragrans aurantiacus* 'Butter Yellow' and 'Orange Supreme' have very fragrant pale or bright orange flowers in the fall.

Turk's Cap
Malvaviscus penduliflorus
Sun, part sun, part shade

Once a common landscape plant, now considered somewhat weedy, this old-fashioned Mexican native continues to add an exotic touch to the summer and fall garden—even in shaded or severely droughty gardens.

FLOWER: Thumb-size red bells hang from every branch, like hibiscus flowers ready to open, but they never do completely. Intensely popular with hummingbirds and butterflies.

PLANT: Large, multi-branched shrub that dies to the ground with freezes but quickly regrows in the spring, with large glossy green oval leaves. Plant must be controlled to prevent escaping into natural areas.

INTERESTING KINDS: A very close but smaller, tidier relative, also called turk's cap or turk's turban (M. *arboreus drummondii*), is native to Florida, with upright flowers and bright red apple-like fall fruits.

Walter's Viburnum
Viburnum obovatum
Sun, part sun, part shade

This Florida native, a 2002 Florida Plant of the Year, is a dense shrub suitable for shady garden barriers, groupings, or specimens in foundation plantings.

FLOWER: Small white flowers in clusters are produced in a heavy cloud over the shrub in the late winter and early spring, followed by red fruits that turn black by fall and are favored by birds.

PLANT: Naturally rounded evergreen shrub in most of Florida (semi-deciduous some winters in northern counties), to seven or more feet tall and four feet wide, with red new growth.

INTERESTING KINDS: Dwarf varieties include 'Densa' and 'Whorle Class'. Sandankwa viburnum (*V. suspensum*) is another very popular spring-blooming viburnum, for hedges to eight feet tall.

Weeping Mary Butterfly Bush
Buddleia lindleyana
Sun or part sun

Although more commonly sold butterfly bushes (the genus is sometimes spelled *Buddleja*) are showier in flower but more sensitive to humidity and soil nematodes, this old-garden passalong plant is dependable and long lived.

FLOWER: Long, thin, cascading flower stems of narrow, purplish violet trumpets hang in clusters up to two feet long. Cutting off spent flower stems forces fast new flower production, but is not as necessary as with other buddleias.

PLANT: Open, graceful, arching branches from sucker-spreading trunks with cinnamon-colored, shedding bark, and glossy willow-like leaves. Can be limbed up for planting underneath.

INTERESTING KINDS: Summer lilac (*B. davidii*) is widely available in many selections, but is often short lived because of root-knot nematode problem. Popular selections include deep purple 'Black Knight', 'Nanho Blue', and white 'Nanho Alba' and 'White Profusion.'

Yesterday, Today, and Tomorrow
Brunfelsia pauciflora (B. grandiflora)
Sun, part sun, part shade

Named as a 2003 Florida Plant of the Year, the flowers fade from purple to lavender pink to white, with some of all three on the plant at all times, giving the plant its common name.

FLOWER: Flat, round, five-petaled disks up to two inches wide are produced all over the plant from spring through summer.

PLANT: Shrubs to eight or ten feet are usually kept smaller with tip pruning. Leaves are oval or lance-shaped, dark green above, light green underneath. Flowers best with regular summer watering.

INTERESTING KINDS: 'Floribunda Compacta' is about two-thirds the size of the more widely-planted 'Floribunda', and has more flowers per shrub. 'Macrantha' ('Magnifica') has much larger flowers (to four inches across) but is not winter hardy in North Florida.

Yucca
Yucca species
Full sun to light shade

Yuccas have a bad rep, but truth is, soft-tipped varieties are neither dangerous nor invasive. Bold forms and flowers are tropical accents that will grow anywhere.

FLOWER: Tall loose clusters of two- to three-inch-wide white bells, spring to fall depending on species; very showy, slightly fragrant, and edible.

PLANT: Spreading rosettes of slender, sword-like leaves to two and a half or more feet long with extremely sharp tips, some stiff and dangerous, others soft and flexible. Some species grow into tall trunks but some are thick mounding clumps of many rosettes. Slow growing at first.

INTERESTING KINDS: One of the most useful is the small Adam's needle (*Y. filamentosa*), especially 'Bright Edge' with white edges and 'Garland's Gold' with a yellow stripe down each leaf.

Other Great Shrubs:

Azalea (*Rhododendron* species) has springtime showy, flattened funnels, single, double, or "hose-in-hose" (one flower stuck inside another), in red, pink, white, orange, mauve, purple, and spotted or streaked combinations. Often troubled by insect pests, water issues, and pH problems. Some types, including the Encore hybrids, rebloom in the fall.

Button Bush (*Cephalanthus occidentalis*) is a very dependable native shrub for low or wet areas, whose round flowers are very fragrant and attractive to bees and butterflies.

Golden Dewdrop

Cassava (*Manihot esculenta*), from which tapioca is made, is a small exotic tree with open hand-shaped leaves that create a very tropical effect. The variegated form is particularly striking.

Dwarf Poinciana (*Caesalpinia pulcherrima*) has among the most exotic flowers found anywhere, but is not reliably hardy in northern counties except along the Gulf Coast.

Elderberry (*Sambucus canadensis*) is a large, spreading, semi-woody herbaceous shrub with dinner-plate-sized masses of white flowers in early summer and large heads of purple fall berries that birds love. Excellent for low, wet areas.

Firethorn (*Pyracantha coccinea*) has clouds of white flowers in the spring and brilliant orange or red berries in tight clusters in the fall and early winter, but the plants have thorns that make it unusable near walks or the lawn.

Florida Leucothoe (*Agarista populifolia*), best for North Florida and the central ridge, is a glossy-leaf native with long, arching branches, often used as an understory plant, shade specimen, or hedge.

Florida Privet, Inkbush, Wild Olive (*Forestiera segregata*) is a very dependable native where a generic green shrub is needed. Can be pruned into a tree form for sun or shade, or sheared into a dense hedge.

Golden Dewdrop (*Duranta erecta* 'Gold Mound'), a 2005 Florida Plant of the Year, is a spreading shrub about two to three feet tall and a little wider, that gives a splash of color to low borders, and holds its yellow-green foliage all summer. The larger-growing 'Sapphire Showers' has purple and white flowers.

Japanese Barberry (*Berberis thunbergii*) is a super-heat-tolerant low-growing shrub with brilliant red foliage that sometimes suffers in hot summer nights and humidity. Very showy around parking lots and dry areas. This plant does besst in North and Central Florida.

Japanese Boxwood (*Buxus microphylla*) is the perfect little naturally round shrub where a bright green gumdrop shape is needed. Best used as an accent or specimen rather than a hedge, where one dying plant can make them all look bad. Nematodes may be a problem in some gardens.

Natal Plum (*Carissa macrocarpa* or *C. grandiflora*) is an informal but naturally rounded shrub, ideal for barriers or foundation plantings, with very showy flowers and fruits. May not be winter hardy in northern counties.

Natal Plum

Oak Leaf Hydrangea (*Hydrangea quercifolia*) is a stunning deciduous shrub for North and parts of Central Florida, with large leaves with gorgeous fall colors and mounds of white flowers and pinkish bracts in late spring to early summer. The woodland native, a 2002 Florida Plant of the Year, requires shade.

Pineapple Guava (*Feijoa sellowiana*) has exotic red and pink flowers and tasty fruits. Regular guava is invasive, but not this one.

Plum Yew (*Cephalotaxus* species) is an underused evergreen shrub that has bright green needles like northern yews (*Taxus*), and can take the heat in all but the southernmost areas of Florida. The prostrate form makes a good evergreen groundcover.

Poinsettia (*Euphorbia pulcherrima*) is perfectly hardy outdoors, even in northern counties, and may even flower if it is not exposed to light at night. A freeze will kill it to the ground, but it will come back the following spring.

Rice Paper Plant (*Tetrapanax papyriferus*) has huge leaves, among the largest foliage plants in the state, and can get very large in shaded gardens. In northern counties it may die back after a sudden or hard freeze, but will survive.

Rose of Sharon or **Althaea** (*Hibiscus syriacus*) is a super hardy, summer-flowering hibiscus that suffers from heat and humidity in South Florida.

Sumac (*Rhus* species), a native that grows into a large colonizing mound with showy flower and fruit clusters and good fall color. Cutleaf sumac (*R. typhina* 'Laciniata') is used by designers in shrub borders and large containers. **Note:** Poison sumac, nearly always found in low, wet, boggy soils, has stubby foliage and white berries.

Sweet Shrub (*Calycanthus floridus*) is a native shade-loving woodland shrub long used in North and Central Florida gardens for its spicy-fragrant burgundy flowers in the late winter and spring.

Thryallis (*Galphimia glauca*) is a very showy, ever-blooming shrub with bright spikes of clear yellow flowers set against handsome, gray-green leaves. Its brittle branches break easily.

White Geiger (*Cordia boissieri*), also known as Texas olive, is a 2000 Florida Plant of the Year. Its white, papery flowers produced all summer are the main reason for growing this large shrub or small tree, which is evergreen in South Florida but deciduous in Central Florida and along the Gulf Coast.

Wild Coffee (*Psychotria nervosa*) is a glossy-leaf native with attractive red berries for shaded gardens in Central and South Florida.

Pineapple Guava

Wild Olive or **Snail Seed** (*Cocculus laurifolius*) a 1999 Florida Plant of the Year, is grown for its cut-flower quality foliage, which is deep glossy green with three prominent veins running the length of each leaf. It is also a good background or hedge plant, but may not be completely hardy in all northern counties.

Quintessence in the Garden

Ever find something that is so simple it can't be improved upon? There's a word for "just right" stuff: quintessence.

It usually does only one thing, but does it so well it would be hard to replace. Like the hand-held pencil sharpener. A spatula can be used for shooing a lizard back outside, but it's mostly for hot skillet stuff—hard to cook without one. Others would be smoke alarm, vacuum cleaner, hairbrush, coffee filter, toilet plunger, TV remote control, and the mouse on my computer. We could get by without them, but they'd be missed.

There is also quintessence in the garden: wheelbarrows, night lighting, leaf blowers, and other labor-saving tools taken for granted. Some are multi-purpose, from five-gallon buckets and red wagons to balls of twine and chicken wire; often they have no moving parts, other than a gardener.

Then there is the little stuff that falls somewhere between necessary and just plain handy, like crunchy perlite that does nothing but lighten potting soils, and an opposable thumb. Some we really don't need, but they do a job well and work on the simplest level. Ideal tools which embody the principles of simplicity and rightness include garden hose, watering can, hose-end water valve, leaf rake, pincushion sprinkler, flat metal file, self-locking plastic cable ties, and, for flower arrangers, a metal "frog" or green oasis blocks.

Garden accessories that go to the heart of gardening without adding clutter to our lives include hummingbird feeders, garden benches, wind chimes, rain gauges, outdoor thermometers, weather vanes, tiki torches, and porch swings.

Some living things carry the simple essence of the gardening spirit. My short list would include gourds, shade trees, seeds, hot peppers, rosemary, and such universally grown flowers as orange daylilies, violas, mother-in-law's tongue, and old roses. And the zebra longwing, Florida's official state butterfly.

These are a mere smattering of "just right, almost can't garden without" items that do only one thing, but do it so well they'd be hard to garden without. In other words, they're quintessential!

STOUTHEARTED Trees

Trees are the big items in your garden. Because they are so dramatic in size and effect, trees provide the most important landscape framework for your garden, apart from your home and other structures. Trees enclose and shade the landscape, and provide nesting places and food for wildlife.

They can also be the most destructive elements, as anyone who suffered the summer hurricanes of 2004 will remember. Choosing trees for their sturdiness—and planting them well so they can be as strong and long-lived as possible—is as important as looking at their flowers or foliage effects. This chapter deals with only a few of the very toughest trees planted in garden-type landscapes. Most make fine specimen or stand-out trees because of their flowers or foliage. Some are easy to work into existing beds; others make good shade for more tender plants, and several are excellent "understory" or "in between" plants.

It's an oddball fact, but a small tree will almost always outgrow a larger tree of the same species if planted at the same time. Choosing a tree that is smaller can also be important both for your wallet and your back. Even if you plant small specimens, keep in mind that trees need elbowroom to grow. Meanwhile, nothing beats a clean layer of natural mulch to make trees "look

right" while protecting the new roots from hot summer sun, cold winter nights, and attacks from lawn mowers and string trimmers. Plus, as leaves and bark decompose, they feed the soil around tree roots in a most natural way.

Protect Your Trees

Just one deep gash on tender bark of a young tree can interfere with food movement from leaves to roots, which causes the tree to suffer for years to come. Prevent this common cause of tree death by mulching around the base, edging with bricks, rocks, or other ornate shield, or planting a groundcover such as liriope. Keep in mind that two or more trees can be "connected" at their bases by a large mulched area, in which small shade-loving shrubs or perennials such as ferns, hosta, monkey grass, or ajuga can be planted. Protect vital roots of mature trees from anything that will cut, compact, or bury them, and avoid over-watering and over-fertilizing, which can force top growth that the roots may not be able to support in strong gusty winds.

Getting Trees in the Ground

There is no need to add too much "stuff" to your soil when planting trees, just enough to get them started. Here are a few quick planting tips for trees:

- Dig a wide hole, not a deep one, "roughing up" the sides and bottom of the hole.
- Loosen tree roots from potting soil, and mix the potting soil with the native sand or soil.
- For balled-and-burlapped trees, bury the top of the burlap so it doesn't wick water away from roots.
- Set the tree so its original soil line is even with or barely higher than the soil around it.
- Fill in around roots with original soil (with the potting soil mixed in).
- Make a ring of soil (not a dome up on the trunk) around the planting site to make watering easier the first year or so.
- Loosely stake new trees for a year or two to keep them from falling over in high wind.
- Cover the planting area with leaves, bark, or other natural mulch.
- Water deeply, not frequently, to encourage roots to grow quickly outwardly and down.

Bald Cypress
Taxodium distichum
Sun or light shade

This tall, narrow, many-twigged deciduous tree is perhaps the single best tree other than palms for hurricane resistance. In spite of its "swamp" reputation, it is fast growing in many soil types, including dry.

FLOWER: This ancient "fossil" tree predates flowering plants, and produces round conifer-type cones.

PLANT: Noted for its straight trunk and dense twiggy growth, the tree can easily reach eighty feet or more, with flexible horizontal branches covered with light green, fern-like leaves that turn rusty red before shedding neatly in the fall.

INTERESTING KINDS: The pond cypress (*T. ascendens*) is similar, with upward-pointing leaflets. 'Prairie Sentinel' is very narrow, only about ten feet wide.

Bay Tree
Laurus nobilis
Sun or light shade

The famous bay leaf used in cooking comes from a sturdy evergreen tree that can be used as a background plant or, because it tolerates pruning very well, used as a topiary, even in a large container. The plant is not fussy about anything except good drainage.

FLOWER: Clusters of small yellow flowers are followed by dark purple berries up to an inch long.

PLANT: The evergreen tree gets up to forty feet tall, with dark green, leathery, aromatic leaves that are oval and up to four inches long. It suckers freely into a multi-stemmed cone, but can be thinned into a specimen or clipped into a dense hedge.

INTERESTING KINDS: 'Saratoga' is more tree-like and has broader leaves than the species.

Bottlebrush

Callistemon citrinus

Sun

Several species of bottlebrush are sold as either large shrubs or small trees. Florida's hummingbirds wish we all grew at least one, and northern visitors will all want to take one home.

FLOWER: Flowering twigs are surrounded with dense spikes of long, bristle-like stamens that look like bottle-brushes. Most are red but some are pale yellow. Woody bead-like seed capsules remain for many months, sometimes years, on old stems.

PLANT: Makes a massive large shrub or can be pruned into a small tree to twenty or twenty-five feet tall. In spite of the thin leaves, these brittle trees do not tolerate gusty winds very well, but recover from breakage fairly quickly.

INTERESTING KINDS: Weeping bottlebrush (*C. viminalis*) grows quickly to twenty-five or more feet tall with hanging branches. Popular, hardier cultivars for North Florida include 'Red Cluster' and 'Texas Scarlet'.

Bottle Tree

Silica transparencii 'Gaudi'

Full sun to dense shade

Originating in ancient Arabia, this specimen migrated to the South to create a dazzling effect that is close to zero-maintenance perfection, while being whimsical and daring.

FLOWER: Small to medium, hollow glass cylinders of clear, amber, green, blue, and occasionally rare red, found on the ends of stems all year. May be hazardous in hurricanes.

PLANT: Upright to eight or ten feet, with many branches.

INTERESTING KINDS: Solid-green or solid-amber bottle trees are edged out by unique cultivars, including 'Milk of Magnesia' (pure cobalt blue), 'Beer Bottle Delight' (delicate blend of greens, browns, and transparent), and 'Kaleidoscope Stroke' (popular multicolor display, often with no particular pattern). A close relative is the CD tree (*Plastic tackysanthemum*) with highly reflective flowers that sway in the breeze.

159

Cherry Laurel
Prunus caroliniana
Sun, part sun, shade

In need of a fast, evergreen tree that thrives on neglect? Don't care if it only lives twenty-five or thirty years? Then the native cherry laurel is perfect. Its many seedlings are easy to pull or to share with neighbors.

FLOWER: Small, creamy-white flowers appear in loose spikes in the spring, making the tree seem to sparkle. Small black autumn fruits are enjoyed by birds.

PLANT: Upright, open, multiple-trunked evergreen tree to forty feet high with shiny, dark-green leaves can be pruned into a single-trunk specimen or sheared into tight evergreen hedge plants.

INTERESTING KINDS: The species makes the best tree, but 'Bright 'n Tight' is a compact large shrub that gets only ten feet high.

Citrus
Citrus species
Sun

Florida's state flower is the orange blossom, and even though disease-related planting bans of citrus are sometimes enforced, especially in South Florida, every well-drained garden should at one time or another include at least one kind of sweet-fruited citrus tree.

FLOWER: Very fragrant white flowers followed by sweet, juicy fruits of various sizes and flavors depending on species and variety.

PLANT: Small, rounded evergreen trees that need a good bit of space for air circulation, and require good drainage. Glossy oval leaves and thorny branches are typical of most.

INTERESTING KINDS: Small-fruited kumquat is one of the easiest for home gardeners, and is the most cold hardy. Orange, mandarin, grapefruit, lime, lemon, calamondin, and citron are also very popular.

Crape Myrtle
Lagerstroemia indica
Full sun to light shade

Who needs Northern lilacs when we have crape myrtles? They are glorious in bloom, and architectural in the winter, especially when underplanted with colorful groundcovers or small evergreen shrubs.

FLOWER: Large, loose, football-sized flower clusters of crinkled white, red, pink, lavender, or striped flowers from early summer to frost. Clusters of round seedpods follow

PLANT: Upright to round small trees, usually with multiple trunks and many branches, with oval leaves up to two inches or more long. Smooth trunks are very showy even in the winter.

INTERESTING KINDS: "Old garden" crape myrtles include lavender 'Muscogee' and coral 'Tuscarora', and the nearly-dwarf purple 'Catawba' and red 'Tonto'. Mildew-resistant hybrids with strongly upright trunks mottled with cinnamon-brown blotches include 'Natchez' (white), 'Biloxi' (light pink), 'Cherokee' (red), and others.

Eastern Red Cedar
Juniperus virginiana
Sun

One of the best small evergreens for poor soils, this common roadside native deserves much wider use as a dependable, fast, long-lived evergreen landscape tree. Can be used as a specimen, hedge, or in a row as a windbreak or noise barrier

FLOWER: Not real flowers, but the plants produce small, bright blue, waxy berry-like fruits used for flavoring gin.

PLANT: Conical, dense evergreen to forty to fifty feet tall or more and half as wide, with dark green, aromatic foliage that is needle-like but consists of many tiny, overlapping scales.

INTERESTING KINDS: 'Skyrocket' is a pencil-thin plant to twenty-five feet tall, used in tight hedges. Southern red cedar (sometimes considered a form of *J. virginiana* and sometimes a separate species, *J. silicicola*) is smaller, less dense, and very tolerant of seaside conditions.

Fig
Ficus carica
Sun or part sun

The true Mediterranean fig tree is a traditional favorite of gardens that have "elbowroom" for it to spread out. Sweet figs harvested in the summer are a special Southern treat.

FLOWER: The rounded "fruits" are actually edible, inverted flowers—look closely inside and see for yourself.

PLANT: Round, mounding tree to thirty feet tall and nearly as wide with several heavy trunks and many suckers. Leaves are large, lobed, and rough textured. More salt tolerant than some experts say. It's easy to control size with pruning.

INTERESTING KINDS: 'Brown Turkey' and 'Celeste' are the two most common varieties, but several others are worth trying, including 'Alma' with sweet amber flesh, and 'LSU Gold' with large, bright yellow, sweet fruits.

Glory Bower
Clerodendrum trichotomum
Sun or light shade

This intensely fragrant small tree can become weedy with suckers and seedlings, but has such showy flowers and fruit it becomes quite a focal point.

FLOWER: Fleshy, waxy, deep pink calyxes support long, white, fragrant flowers in the summer; as flowers shed, the calyxes remain to cup metallic blue-green fruits well into fall.

PLANT: Drought-tolerant tree to fifteen or more feet tall and nearly as wide has hairy, oval leaves up to five inches long and nearly as wide. Root suckers can be cut off and the tree pruned to a single trunk. Underplant with groundcovers to hide leggy stems.

INTERESTING KINDS: 'Carnival' and 'Variegata' both have white-edged leaves.

Golden Rain Tree
Koelreuteria paniculata
Sun or light shade

This somewhat weedy tree, which can be controlled easily with regular pulling or cutting of seedlings, is a mainstay for low-maintenance landscapes. It thrives on little or no care, and has several seasons of interest.

FLOWER: Very showy foot-long clusters of yellow flowers turn to reddish fruit capsules that become papery as they mature to light brown; the pods are used in floral arrangements.

PLANT: Rounded tree to forty feet tall and nearly as wide, with ferny compound leaves that start out purplish, turn bright green in the summer, and have yellow fall color.

INTERESTING KINDS: The species is a very dependable tree, but 'Rose Lantern' has rose-pink seed capsules, and 'Fastigiata' gets twenty-five feet tall but only three or four feet wide.

Italian Cypress
Cupressus sempervirens
Sun

Talk about attention getting—this extremely thin evergreen shrub looks like a giant exclamation point. Very important as an accent, and tolerant of salt, drought and high winds. Works well in classical landscapes and highly stylized contemporary ones as well.

FLOWER: None, but can have cones up to one and one half inches long.

PLANT: Evergreen column to fifty or more feet high and only five or six feet wide, with juniper-like foliage and good drought tolerance. Susceptible to spider mites, especially in hot summer weather, that browns older foliage.

INTERESTING KINDS: 'Glauca' is blue green; 'Swane's Golden' has yellowish new growth. A similar plant is 'Skyrocket' juniper (*Juniperus chinensis* or *J. virginiana*), which can tolerate more heat and humidity in South Florida.

163

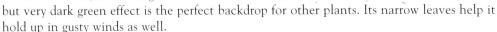

Japanese or Southern Yew
Podocarpus macrophyllus
Sun or part sun

This imposing upright evergreen is a major hedge, accent, or topiary tree for all of Florida, where its generic but very dark green effect is the perfect backdrop for other plants. Its narrow leaves help it hold up in gusty winds as well.

FLOWER: Neither the yellow male catkins nor pale greenish black fruits are showy.

PLANT: Upright evergreen to forty or more feet tall with very narrow leaves to four inches long. Yellow-green new leaves contrast against darker older foliage. Very easily pruned into topiaries or espaliered against tall buildings.

INTERESTING KINDS: 'Maki', sometimes called "shrubby yew pine," gets up to fifteen feet tall, and makes a good large container specimen.

Jerusalem Thorn or Palo Verde
Parkinsonia aculeata
Full sun

If you never want to water again, this is your tree. Its airy, "desert" look complements prairie wildflowers and cacti, and is dramatic against a building in a hot, dry site.

FLOWER: Showy yellow flowers in loose clusters on six- to seven-inch stems that hang down, produced in spring and after rains in the summer; followed by long bean pods..

PLANT: Fast-growing but unpredictable form to twenty-five or more feet tall with yellow-green bark and zig-zag thorny branches that are useful in dried flower arrangements. Leaves are sparse, with many tiny leaflets that shed in drought or cold weather.

INTERESTING KINDS: Only the species is available.

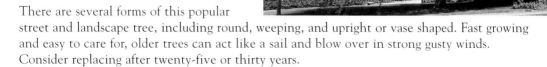

Lacebark or Chinese Elm
Ulmus parvifolia
Sun or light shade

There are several forms of this popular street and landscape tree, including round, weeping, and upright or vase shaped. Fast growing and easy to care for, older trees can act like a sail and blow over in strong gusty winds. Consider replacing after twenty-five or thirty years.

FLOWER: Greenish yellow or reddish in the summer, not showy.

PLANT: Fast-growing to fifty or more feet tall with oval, pointed, leathery green leaves (evergreen in South Florida) and beautiful mottled, patchy bark on the trunks of older specimens, very showy in the winter.

INTERESTING KINDS: 'Athena' gets about thirty feet tall and is rounded; 'Allee' is much taller, upright, perfect as a street tree; 'Drake' is somewhat weeping and widely sold.

Lilac Chaste Tree
Vitex agnus-castus
Full sun or very light shade

Vitex is an old-garden plant that is making a huge comeback as a specimen plant when limbed up near a patio or along a sidewalk, with summer flowers attractive to bees, butterflies, and hummingbirds.

FLOWER: Upright panicles to nearly a foot long crusted with small blue, lavender, pink, or white flowers, produced from late spring into midsummer or later

PLANT: Small rounded, umbrella-like tree, multi-trunked with grayish brown bark and many branches of dense and aromatic leaves (used in ancient times as an herbal treatment) that look like marijuana, for those who notice such things.

INTERESTING KINDS: 'Abbeville Blue' or 'Rosea' are to me more attractive than either of the two common white varieties *V. agnus-castus* forma *alba* and 'Silver Spire'.. The new cultivar 'Shoal Creek' is gaining in popularity across the state.

Loquat
Eriobotrya japonica
Sun or part sun

This bold, wooly-looking round tree, also called Japanese plum, has an unusual habit of flowering in the fall, and fruiting in the winter and spring. It is striking as an accent, but especially choice if highlighted against a tall wall or building.

FLOWER: Interesting clusters of small, dull white flowers are fragrant but not very showy, appearing in the fall. Orange, many-seeded, sweet fruits up to two inches long ripen in the winter and spring.

PLANT: Thirty-foot, rounded evergreen tree with foot-long leathery leaves with deep netting and veins that are brown and wooly underneath.

INTERESTING KINDS: Many that are sold are inferior seedlings; for fruit production, plant named varieties such as 'Gold Nugget', 'Macbeth', or late-ripening 'Thales'.

Magnolia
Magnolia grandiflora
Full sun or moderate shade

The most glorious native tree of the South has huge, fragrant flowers and dense evergreen leaves. The leaf litter problem can be easily solved.

FLOWER: Tulip-shaped white buds open into fragrant bowls of pure white with yellow stamens, followed by showy red berry-like fruits emerging from bristly pods.

PLANT: Upright evergreen tree has foot-long, deep glossy green foliage with fuzzy brown undersides. Leaf litter is a problem that can be "cleaned up" by underplanting with groundcovers like liriope.

INTERESTING KINDS: Avoid seedlings and choose named varieties. 'Little Gem' is a compact, upright, long-blooming dwarf to narrow-type to thirty feet that fits in many landscapes as a specimen, accent, or hedge; larger kinds such as 'Alta' and 'Brackens Brown Beauty' can be huge. 'D. D. Blanchard' is popular with landscapers.

Oak

Quercus species
Sun to part sun

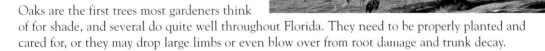

Oaks are the first trees most gardeners think of for shade, and several do quite well throughout Florida. They need to be properly planted and cared for, or they may drop large limbs or even blow over from root damage and trunk decay.

FLOWER: Hanging catkins appear with early leaves, followed by acorns that are more messy than ornamental.

PLANT: Tall, wide, evergreen or deciduous trees that provide much-needed shade, with wide-ranging roots that should be protected from digging, paving, and other limiting factors. Leaf litter is sometimes a problem, but is easily solved by groundcovers planted underneath.

INTERESTING KINDS: Evergreen live oak (*Q. virginiana*) needs occasional limb thinning; laurel oak (*Q. laurifolia*) grows naturally down to the Everglades, but is brittle. Sand live oak (*Q. germinate*) is very good for near beaches, and *Q. shumardii* has red fall color that drops quickly.

Pine

Pinus species
Sun to part sun

There are a handful of pines that are surprisingly hardy throughout Florida, from north to south. They are excellent wind screens, and provide light shade for understory plants such as azaleas and gingers.

FLOWER: Yellow "candles" in the spring, brown cones in the fall.

PLANT: Tall, narrow, evergreen with tufts of narrow, deep green "needles" that fall into useful "pine straw" mulch. Roots are shallow and should not be cut or crushed, or even driven over.

INTERESTING KINDS: The best all-around pine for the entire state would be slash pine (*P. elliotii*), which reaches sixty to eighty feet tall in most gardens and has attractive cones. Sand or scrub pine (*P. clausa*) and spruce pine (*P. glabra*) are smaller but equally versatile. Long-leaf pine (*P. palustris*) is a very important native.

Purple Orchid Tree
Bauhinia variegata
Sun to part sun

Surprisingly cold-hardy to the lower 20s, this species of a very flamboyant genus makes a great small tree in protected areas in northern Florida, and a curbside or street tree elsewhere.

FLOWER: Broad-petaled, light pink to orchid purple flowers are up to three inches wide from late winter to mid-spring, followed by a huge crop of messy beans that can be left on or pruned off. Winter freezes can keep the tree from flowering the following summer.

PLANT: Prune and stake this many-stemmed large shrub early in its life so it will grow into an attractive tree up to twenty-five or more feet tall. Unusual twin leaves are actually lobes on a single leaf.

INTERESTING KINDS: 'Candida' has white flowers. Brazilian orchid tree (*B. candicans*) can tolerate a little cold weather along northeastern and northwestern coastal areas.

Purple Trumpet Tree
Tabebuia impetiginosa 'Ipe'
Sun to part sun

Most of the beautiful members of this tropical genus are for Florida's southern counties, but 'Ipe', a 2004 Florida Plant of the Year selection, has tolerated temperatures down into the upper teens.

FLOWER: The two- to three-inch-long lavender-pink flowers with yellow centers appear in clusters in early spring, covering the bare branches, often reblooming in the summer. May take several years to reach flowering size or maturity, but worth the wait!

PLANT: Deciduous tree to twenty-five feet tall, with smooth, dark green, palmately compound leaves and furrowed light gray bark. Very tolerant of coastal conditions but does very well in a warm sunny site away from the beach.

INTERESTING KINDS: Yellow or pink trumpet trees are equally showy but less cold hardy.

Red Maple

Acer rubrum

Sun, part sun, part shade

Fall colors in Florida? You bet, when you plant this tidy tree that is native even to South Florida! Its preferred site is low and moist (another common name is swamp maple) but it will tolerate normal seasons while taking wet summers very well.

FLOWER: Reddish flowers appear in December and January, followed by red-winged fruits that sail away like mini-helicopters.

PLANT: Fast-growing generic oval "tree" shape to sixty or seventy feet tall and half as wide, with gray-green foliage.

INTERESTING KINDS: 'Florida Flame', 'Autumn Flame', and 'October Glory' have outstanding red fall colors in North and Central Florida. 'Trilobum', native to South Florida (but not the Keys), has three pointy leaf lobes and red leaf stems.

Soapberry

Sapindus species

Sun

Excellent for small yards, this round-topped small tree grows well in adverse conditions, and a soapy lather can be made from its berries. Not widely sold, but an excellent fast shade tree for small gardens

FLOWER: Tiny yellowish white flowers appear in ten-inch-long clusters in the early summer, followed by deep yellow fruits that turn black by late fall.

PLANT: Spreading tree to thirty feet tall and nearly as wide, with leaves divided into many leaflets. Tolerant of poor, dry soil and wind. This tree self-seeds readily, and can be a real control problem for some gardeners.

INTERESTING KINDS: Florida soapberry (*S. marginatus*) has white flowers in the spring and golden yellow fall colors. 'Narrow Leaf' has finer-textured, narrower leaves.

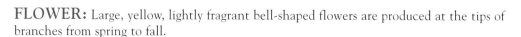

Yellow Bells or Yellow Elder
Tecoma stans
Sun or part sun

This Florida native was named a 2005 Florida Plant of the Year for its reliable, all-season flowers.

FLOWER: Large, yellow, lightly fragrant bell-shaped flowers are produced at the tips of branches from spring to fall.

PLANT: Small tree to over twenty feet tall with light green compound leaves. Can be pruned into a shrub with light pruning, especially in northern counties where a sudden or hard freeze can kill the plant to the ground, from which it will quickly return the next spring.

INTERESTING KINDS: 'Gold Star' is completely reliable and blooms constantly throughout the warm season. *Tecoma stans angustata*, a Texas native, tolerates down to 10 degrees, and needs less water and fertilizer than the species.

Wax Myrtle
Myrica cerifera
Sun or part sun

This North Florida native is often limbed up into a small specimen tree, and makes a fantastic filler plant under pines and other taller trees.

FLOWER: Blooms are not very showy, but female plants bear waxy, grayish fruits in dense clusters along stems, which are used to make "bayberry" candles.

PLANT: Wide, spreading shrub with narrow, olive-green leaves grows quickly to fifteen or more feet tall unless pruned. Brittle limbs often break in high winds, but quickly resprout.

INTERESTING KINDS: 'Luray' is a compact selection that gets only about four or five feet tall and wide. The dwarf wax myrtle (*M. pumila*) is almost a completely different plant, growing to only around three feet tall but spreading widely by suckers.

Other Good Trees:
(N: Best for North Florida, C: Central Florida, S: South Florida):

Avocado (*Persea americana*) large-size shade tree with showy greenish purple fruit. CS

Camphor Tree (*Cinnamomum camphora*) invasive large evergreen street tree. CS

Catalpa (*Catalpa bignonioides*) large-leaves, showy flowers, long beans, giant Catalpa moth larvae host. NC

Chinaberry (*Melia azedarach*) considered old fashioned and invasive, hard to find. NC

Ficus (*Ficus benjamina, F. elastica, F. microcarpa*) evergreen tropical trees with milky sap and hanging aerial roots. S

Frangipani (*Plumeria* species) large leaves, exotic, highly fragrant "lei" flowers in white, red, pink, yellow. CS

Fringe Tree (*Chionanthus virginicus*) native with clouds of small white spidery flowers as spring leaves emerge. NC

Ginkgo (*Ginkgo biloba*) interesting foliage with bright yellow fall colors. NC

Gumbo-Limbo (*Buersera simaruba*) old time favorite canopy tree. S

Jacaranda (*Jacaranda mimosifolia*) fernlike leaves and incredibly showy clusters of lavender blue flowers. CS

Japanese Magnolia (*Magnolia × soulangeana*) showy fragrant, saucer-shaped flowers of white, pink, maroon, or combinations in late winter before foliage. NC

Pawpaw

Go Native

Many great trees are native to Florida, including: American holly, bald cypress, eastern red cedar, loblolly bay (*Gordonia*), persimmon, red maple, river birch, magnolia, oaks, pawpaw, redbud, sweet gum, sycamore, wax myrtle, red buckeye, fringe tree, catalpa, sweetbay magnolia, sassafras, cherry laurel, and pine.

Redbud

Japanese Persimmon (*Diospyros kaki*) large orange fall fruit. NC

Jujube (*Ziziphus jujuba*) summer date-like fruit. NCS

Loblolly Bay (*Gordinia lasianthus*) is a small native tree with small white magnolia-like flowers in the spring. NC

Mango (*Mangifera indica*) favorite shade tree with showy flowers and fruit. S

Marlberry (*Ardisia escallonioides*) small shade tree with attractive foliage and berries. S

Norfolk Island Pine (*Auaucaria heterophylla*) exotic conifer with outstretched tiers of limbs with deep green leaves. CS

Ornamental Pear (*Pyrus calleryana*) spring flowers and fall colors better in North Florida, not good in gusty winds. NC

Papaya (*Carica papaya*) hollow-stemmed tree-like perennial, big palm-like leaves, large fruits growing on trunks. S

Pawpaw (*Asimina triloba*) native with egg-size summer "custard apple" fruit, fall color, butterfly host. NCS

Pigeon Plum (*Coccoloba diversifolia*) very tough native with shiny leaves for hedges, screens, understory. CS

Red Buckeye (*Aesculus pavia*) native woodland tree with coarse leaves and very showy red spring flowers. Attracts hummingbirds. NC

Redbud (*Cercis canadensis*) very showy native with pinkish red flowers in late winter, heart-shaped leaves. NC

Red Cassia (*Cassia roxburghii*) small tree with ferny leaves and exotic, red, pea-like summer flowers. NCS

River Birch (*Betula nigra*) excellent often multi-trunk native with papery bark, very good hurricane survivability. NC

AN INSTANT "TREE" IS EASIER THAN YOU'D THINK—if you consider about how easy a large deck umbrella can be. One large-diameter post—at least ten feet high—set into the ground, then planted with a vine, can create the same effect as a "real" tree. Setting up a two-post arbor—again, at least ten feet high, using six-by-six posts instead of cheap four-by-four's—is only a little more expensive, with nearly twice the appeal.

Best for Beginners:

- Bald Cypress
- Cedar
- Cherry Laurel
- Crape Myrtle
- Drake Elm
- Hollies
- Lilac Chaste Tree
- Oaks
- Magnolia 'Little Gem'
- Red Maple
- River Birch

Kinda Tricky:

- Bottlebrush
- Citrus
- Fringe Tree
- Fruit Trees
- Italian Cypress
- Jerusalem Thorn
- Loquat
- Trumpet Tree

Royal Poinciana, Flamboyant Tree (*Delonix regia*) incredibly beautiful flowers, doubly fern-like leaves. S

Sassafras (*Sassafras albidum*) colony-forming, root beer bark, fall color, butterfly host. NCS

Sea Grape (*Cocculoba uvifera*) huge-leaved coast favorite with clusters of edible fruit. CS

Spicy Jatropha (*Jatropha integerrima*) large tropical heart-shaped leaves, clusters of scarlet flowers. CS

Sweetbay Magnolia (*Magnolia virginiana*) deciduous magnolia, small leaves, small flowers. NC

Sweet Gum (*Liquidambar styraciflua*) fast growing with good fall colors, prickly seed balls a nuisance. NC

Royal Poinciana

Sycamore (*Platanus occidentalis*) fast growing, large-leaf shade tree. NC

Tung Oil Tree (*Aleurites fordii*) showy pinkish white flowers, large leaves, oily nuts, can reseed prolifically. NCS

Umbrella Tree (*Schefflera actinophylla*) lush tropical tree with red flower spikes, banned in South Florida. CS

Yellow Poinciana, Yellow Flame Tree (*Peltophorum pterocarpum*) ferny leaves, showy spikes of yellow flowers. CS

Bugs and Blights, Oh, My

"If you can't fix it, flee it, or fight it, then flow with it."

Sooner, rather than later, all gardeners have to deal with bugs and blights and things that bump in the garden. A couple of generations ago all we could do was "go with the flow"—plant enough for everyone, including the pests, and replant as needed. Then, in just the last half-century, we got into a race to find ever-more-potent chemical solutions, a pie-in-the-sky "shotgun" approach that often caused more problems than it solved. Now most of the "good ones" are gone, victims of their own potency or overuse.

Nowadays, the term "pest control" no longer means total eradication; it means "abatement"—knocking down the worst, and living with a certain amount of pest damage. And a safer, more moderate approach is emerging, called "Integrated Pest Management" or IPM. It simply involves using several different practices chosen from a wide array of easy options:

- Choose pest-resistant plants to begin with, or replace problem plants.
- Plant well—good soil preparation goes a long ways towards having healthy plants.
- Fertilize lightly, not heavily (overfed plants are weak and tender).
- Water deeply and infrequently, and only when plants really need it.
- Spend time in the garden, so you can see problems when they first appear.
- Remove diseased plants or plant parts, or damage that can lead to diseases.
- Encourage beneficial insects, birds, even spiders and lizards, which eat pests.
- Hand pick or wash insects off plants with soapy water.
- Use traps, baits, repellents, or other non-toxic measures.
- Learn to live with a moderate amount of damage.

As a last resort, choose the least toxic material—natural or chemical—for the specific pest, on the specific plant, and use it only as directed. Read and follow directions.

These guidelines are nothing new—just good gardening practices used by gardeners for many centuries. They're still worth following— maybe now more than ever.

Deus ex Machina—No Last-Minute Bailout

Anyone remember the old "How to Serve Man" Twilight Zone program in which aliens came to Earth with all sorts of human-helping powers, before their manual was "outed" as a cookbook? What seem like miraculous bailouts often become horror stories.

Same with gardening. Whenever a new, seemingly spontaneous "cure" comes along for weeds, animals, bugs, or blights, a subtle but high price seems to come with it.

My wife got me on this line of thinking as we reminisced about high school days, and brought up a phrase I somehow missed in class (go figure—she was a member of the National Honor Society; I was a classic "underachiever"). The phrase is *deus ex machina*, or "god from the machine."

In this stage device, often used in Greek and Roman dramas, an apparently unsolvable crisis is solved at the last minute by the intervention of a "god" actor descending onstage by a wire suspended from the ceiling, or some other elaborate piece of equipment. It's the oldest version of being "saved by the cavalry."

I've been thinking about this "pie in the sky" approach to gardening. It took us a couple of generations to catch on that almost every new-fangled pest-eradicating chemical causes terrible, unforeseen hits on "non-target" species of plants, birds, or other wildlife, and sometimes ruins drinking water supplies. And the pests outmaneuver to come back with a vengeance (especially since some of their controls were eliminated in the process). There are no universal controls for deer, mice, voles, squirrels, slugs, groundhogs, or other furry or noxious pests. Few plants are totally resistant to them; fences, netting, wire mulches, and other barriers are cumbersome and ugly; poisons, baits, and repellants usually fail in the long run and kill "non-target" species as well. Sorry!

Truth is, gardening is a constant bailing of a very leaky boat. Wishful thinking won't make nature stop trying to fix itself: First come the weeds (nature's shock troops, called "pioneer species" by eco-gardeners), then birds that bring seed of larger plants to push the inexorable succession toward the old forest we cut down to make room for turf, potato patches, and daylilies (whose only contribution to wildlife is aphids).

Heaven didn't put lawns or hybrid tea roses here—we did, by enslaving and breeding plants from afar. And we wonder why they chafe and suffer and rebel from our domination!

When last-minute scientific breakthroughs fail to arrive, we should garden smarter by doing less counter-intuitive stuff like planting high-maintenance or pest-predictable plants, and by choosing tried-and-true plants that at worst can survive the onslaughts and at best will thrive in the face of adversity.

TERRIFIC
Tropicals

Most of us learned at an early age how to grow plants in pots, from the first time a school teacher showed us how to put a bean seed in a milk carton. We learned to give it a little sunshine, some water when it got dry, and a little "plant food" to help it grow.

Then it usually died, which set us up for expecting failure with poinsettias and African violets given to us as gifts. And when we or a family member came home from the hospital with one of those mixed pots of baby tropical plants—usually a heart-leaf philodendron, a small palm, a mother-in-law's tongue, and a prayer plant—the prayer plant quickly gave up the ghost. Then without realizing it, we began learning about tough plants, because that mother-in-law's tongue survived, and the heart-leaf philodendron vine began spreading all around the window. Those simple plants taught us that some potted creatures actually thrive in the low-light, low-humidity, cool-temperature spaceship environments we call home. And quite a few are perfectly happy outdoors in our gardens also, usually in the shade since they naturally occur as jungle understory plants.

Florida—Not All Subtropical

In spite of the palms, Norfolk pines, and bromeliads we see everywhere, and the tropical plantings around service stations and shopping malls, most of Florida is a tricky place for growing tropical plants—unlike Hawaii, which is entirely in the tropics. Even in Orlando and Tampa, tropical plants can get nipped from a sudden frost; only a few are ground-hardy in northern areas of the Panhandle, while some are considered invasive weeds, even banned outright in parts of South Florida. Still, many popular plants from the tropics are grown outdoors in pots than can be brought indoors if need be for a night or two. This chapter highlights some of the toughest, easiest to grow, longest-lived tropical plants that are hardy in most of the state, or grown as potted plants everywhere.

Environmental and Cultural Needs

Location, location, location! Most of these plants grow well in widely varying conditions, but do best—especially those grown in containers—if provided

with three basic conditions: bright indirect light, humidity, and protection from freezing. Beyond that, how you take care of your plants will determine the difference between their thriving and merely surviving. Water, fertilizer, and occasional repotting are about all they need.

Water "as needed"—too wet is worse than too dry; variations in environmental conditions, plant type, pot size, potting soil type, and the amount of fertilizer used will cause plants to grow at different rates and need water in varying amounts. Fertilize plants very little at a time—I use a good timed-release fertilizer (the long-lasting fertilizer beads) once in the spring, then occasionally hit the plants with a light shot of liquid plant food containing "trace minerals" (iron, zinc, calcium, etc., listed on the side of the container). **Note:** Use plant foods at one-half the recommended strength—the directions on the containers indicate the absolute highest application amounts, which are simply not necessary for good plant growth.

Repotting should be done when plants have been in the same worn-out potting soil for years or when the plant has gotten too big for its pot. My personal potting soil recipe, which I came up with while researching various mixes in college, holds up a long time, keeps plants upright in the pots, stays moist without staying wet, and holds nutrients so they don't wash out too quickly. It is easy to make and inexpensive; I mix it on the driveway and store it in a plastic garbage can.

Ingredients: One part cheap potting soil and one part finely ground pine bark mulch. That's it. The bark allows good water and air penetration; the potting soil holds moisture and nutrients. Sometimes I put a few rocks in the bottom of the pots to help keep top-heavy plants from tipping over.

👍 Best for Beginners:

- Airplane Plant
- Asparagus Fern
- Chinese Evergreen
- Devil's Backbone
- Dwarf Schefflera
- Heart-Leaf Philodendron
- Rubber Tree
- Snake Plant

Kinda Tricky: 👎

- Bird's Nest Fern
- Brazilian Plume
- Bromeliads
- Croton
- Orchids
- Weeping Fig

179

Aluminum Plant

Pilea cadierei

Part shade

Semi-hardy, many-stemmed shrub, fast growing to two feet or more tall. Pointy-oval, quilted-textured dark green leaves have bold silver markings between the veins. Pinch it back to make it bushier. It can be used in masses as a showy groundcover for the shade. Flowers are very small and not showy. 'Minima' is less than half the size of the species. Other common *Pilea* species include artillery fern (*P. microphylla*) that spreads rapidly in shade by seed, and creeping Charlie (*P. nummularifolia*), a cascading vine used often in hanging baskets.

Baby Rubber Plant

Peperomia obtusifolia

Part shade or shade

Bushy, multi-stem plant to a foot or more tall and wide with succulent stems and smooth, glossy deep green leaves, up to four inches long with a notch near the end. Flowers are small but on interesting cord-like spikes. Very sensitive to frost damage. 'Variegata' has wide, irregular creamy white leaf margins. Other *Peperomia* species include watermelon peperomia (*P. sandersii*) and emerald ripple (*P. caperata*).

Bird's Nest Fern

Asplenium nidus

Part shade or shade

The upright, outward-growing fronds of this rosette-forming fern are striking in shaded gardens for their green-apple color and un-fernlike, undivided shape, which can get two to three or more feet long and eight inches wide. Must be protected from heavy rains and wind, and frost, but well worth the trouble for lightening up tropical settings.

Bromeliads
Many different types
Sun or part shade

The plants in the large "pineapple" family are mostly stemless with clustered leaves, many of which are handsomely marked. Flower clusters often have colorful, long-lasting bracts. Most are epiphytes (grow in trees) while others are terrestrial (grow on the ground or well-drained potting soil). Those that hold water in their central cups should not be kept wet if grown indoors, or the water can stagnate and cause rot. Some of the more commonly grown bromeliads are briefly described below—there are many, many others.

Aechmea bromeliads grow with the bases of their leaves forming urns or rosettes that can hold water, and grow best in fast-draining potting soil. No need to keep the central vase filled with water, or rot may occur.

Ananas comosus is the familiar pineapple, a terrestrial bromeliad that is easy to grow as a plant but may take two or more years to produce a flowering (fruiting) stem. Grow plants from tops cut off mature fruits, rooted in shallow water. The variegated form is very showy.

Billbergia species are usually tall, urn-shaped epiphytes with variegated, banded, mottled, colorful foliage and cutting-quality flowers. *B. nutans* is a cold-hardy groundcover even in the Panhandle Easy to divide.

Cryptanthus bromeliads are commonly called "earth stars" for their flattened rosettes of narrow leaves usually banded or striped. They grow best in very porous potting soils.

Neoregelia species are striking epiphytes that grow as rosettes of stiff leaves with white or blue flowers above the cup of foliage, which will hold water. The central portion often turns rosy red. Spiny edged leaves can have red spots or leaf tips.

Tillandsia species are mostly epiphytes, some with very showy flowers. The most common natives are Spanish moss (*T. usineoides*) and ball moss (*T. recurvata*).

181

Chinese Evergreen
Aglaeonema species
Medium to low light

Chinese evergreen thrives in offices and airports where all other plants slowly waste away in the low light and low humidity. But they also make superb additions to the home garden potted plant palette. Small, canna-like plants have several sturdy upright stems of narrow, sword-like leaves up to a foot or more long and glossy, often patterned. Beautiful tricolor 'Silverado' was named a 2004 Florida Plant of the Year.

Chinese Hibiscus
Hibiscus rosa-sinensis
Sun or part sun

One of the standard tropical plants for large pots or specimens, hedges, or even large bedding plants, this deep green or variegated but glossy-leaf species will tolerate frost, but not freezes. Its single or double flowers, smooth or ruffled, are large, up to eight inches across, and are available in an astounding array of colors and combinations, including red, white, pink, apricot, orange, and yellow, but no true blues or purples. There are simply too many great varieties to name even my own favorite. Pinching stem tips helps keep plants blooming.

Croton
Codiaeum variegatum
Full sun—the more the better

In Africa I saw this plant at nearly every doorstep, in the hottest, sunniest part of the yard. The wavy, foot-long, leathery leaves, sometimes wide like a rubber tree or very narrow and curly, are glossy and splashed in every imaginable combination of green, yellow, orange, pink, purple, red, and bronze—the more sun it gets, the more color it has. It will not tolerate cold, so has to be kept in pots and moved indoors for winter in northern Florida counties.

Dracaena

Dracaena species

Bright to moderately low light

The common corn plant (*D. fragrans*) is often sold as tiered, multiple-stemmed specimens, with each stem up to three inches in diameter and topped with a large whorl of long, downward curving leaves, each up to three feet long and four inches wide. 'Massangeana' has a broad yellow stripe down the center of each leaf. Others are smaller with thinner leaves, usually formed as topknots on tall arching stems. Ribbon dracaena (*D. sanderiana*) is small and white- or yellow-variegated. The popular "Chinese good luck bamboo" is simply a ribbon dracaena leaned at different angles during production to produce twisted or spiral stems.

Dumb Cane

Dieffenbachia species

Bright to medium light, tolerates low light

Know someone who talks too much? *Dieffenbachia* (dee-fen-BACH-e-uh) will shut them up—swallowing even a small amount of the plant's sap can paralyze the voice box, leaving a person unable to talk for hours (not a nice thing to do, so I'm not recommending it). Bold, wide, pointed leaves can be striking with variegations, stripes, edging, and spots of white, yellow, chartreuse, or cream. Tall plants can be cut back severely to force strong new growth near the base; the cut-off portions are easily rooted.

Dwarf Schefflera

Schefflera arboricola

Bright to moderately low light

This tidy little shrub, not invasive like the taller umbrella schefflera, has leathery, deep green, hand-sized, many-fingered leaves, sometimes variegated. The plant tends to become branchy and quite leggy in low light, but pruning thickens it up again. 'Gold Capella' has deep green, shiny, oval leaves with contrasting intensely yellow variegation. These heat-tolerant plants can be used as large bedding plants or potted specimens. 'Trinette' was named a Florida Plant of the Year.

Hawaiian Ti
Cordyline terminalis
Part shade or shade

This gaudy potted plant, hardy outdoors in Central and South Florida, is often used as a showy understory planting where hot colors are needed and acceptable. Long, pointed leaves are fairly wide in the center, and usually striped with red, yellow, or near-magenta, and the thin dracaena-like stems are very easy to root in sections. A larger, hardier giant species (*C. australis*) has several very colorful cultivars. Hawaiians often cook food wrapped in Ti leaves.

Heliconia
Heliconia psittacorum
Sun, part sun, part shade

Both beautiful and bizarre, this plant has the foliage of ginger or canna, and arching stems of flowers and bracts that together are shaped like lobster claws or parrot beaks, in red, yellow, orange, pink, lavender, and green. Most are not hardy in North Florida, in protected areas with lots of mulch. 'Golden Torch' is simple and reminds me of the wild "bird's foot" heliconias of South America; 'Lady Di' has a striking combination of red and yellow; many others are available.

Ixora
Ixora coccinea
Sun or part sun

The commonly-planted "jungle flame" is a shrub in South Florida and a freeze-tender but sometimes root-hardy perennial farther north—a durable mainstay flowering plant of summer. Generic green foliage can be sheared or pruned, but is constantly topped with very showy dense, rounded clusters of red, orange, pink, or yellow. 'Nora Grant' is the most popular large pink cultivar, but also try 'Orange Sherbet' or 'Pink Pixie'.

Orchids
Many genera and hybrids between them
Bright to moderately low light

With over 17,000 species of orchids, perhaps the largest family in the plant kingdom, there naturally has to be at least one for every Florida gardener. Nearly all of the "epiphytes" (air plants) are grown in pots or small hanging baskets filled with bark, or wired onto "rafts" of wood. A few "terrestrial" kinds are grown in very well-drained potting soil mixed with bark.

Getting started with orchids is easy—just buy a few, and keep them humid, moist (not wet), and lightly fed with liquid plant food. Expect at least some to survive. Commercial orchid soils and fertilizers take away a lot of the guesswork.

Best Orchids for Beginners:

Cattleya orchids are among the most popular for their ease of culture and large, very fragant "corsage" flowers. Dark growing conditions turn the leaves dark green but makes them soft.

Dendrobium orchids need some direct sunshine; some types have a nearly dormant winter period during which they lose their leaves and need very little water.

Phaelanopsis, the "moth" orchid, has thick, leathery leaves and long sprays of large flowers up to six-inches wide. They are terrestrial, and need a well-drained potting soil.

Cymbidium orchids are terrestrial (grow in containers) with long, narrow, grass-like leaves and long-lasting flowers on arching spikes; they can tolerate very cool weather.

Oncidium orchids include a wide range of terrestrial orchids, some native to Florida, that grow in pots or in tree hollows.

Peace Lily
Spathiphyllum species
Moderate to deep shade

The large, dark leaves and pure white flowers of this extremely shade-tolerant calla lily relative cause it to be nearly overused as an indoor plant. It is everywhere, especially in airports, malls, and office buildings, and fills in nicely in shady garden spots, especially in containers. The plant wilts conveniently when it needs watering. For continuous new growth of both foliage and flowers, fertilize lightly every few waterings.

Philodendron
Philodendron species
Bright to medium light

Grown for their glossy leaves, this diverse but durable genus of tropical vines and sub-shrubs are includes some of the most common houseplants in the country, and most are winter hardy outdoors in all parts of Florida. Very few gardeners ever see a philodendron flower, which is a creamy white, calla-like spathe hidden within the foliage canopy. The foliage is glossy, slick (almost rubbery), and durable even in low humidity. Most grow best in bright but indirect light. Split-leaf philodendron (*P. bipinnatifidum*, formerly *P. selloum*) has huge, elephant-ear leaves, deeply divided almost to the midrib, produced from a stocky, shrub-like trunk with incredibly strong aerial roots used for support. It and a near relative (*Monstera deliciosa*, which often has holes in the leaves like Swiss cheese) can get six to eight feet tall, with leaves up to three feet long. 'Xanadu' is a super-tough "dwarf" form used in mass plantings, groundcovers, or as a potted specimen for low-light, low-humidity, breezy spots. 'Royal Queen' has spade-shaped leaves with deep red coloration. Many other cultivars are available.

Rubber Tree
Ficus elastica
Full sun to moderate light

Sturdy and bold, this tropical giant is barely hardy outdoors in northern counties, and is often grown as a large potted plant. Glossy, flattened football-shaped leaves can be green, burgundy, or have red stems and midribs; a variegated form is especially beautiful for lower light areas where a bold, durable splash is needed. Pruning forces new stems to emerge at the cut, which thickens the plants into shrubs. Fiddle-leaf fig (*F. lyrata*) has larger, fiddle-shaped leaves.

Shrimp Plant
Justicia brandegeeana
(Beleperone guttata)
Sun or part sun

Light green foliage on this small shrub contrasts with the curved or drooping, three- to six-inch, jointed-looking flower clusters which are made of overlapping bronze-red bracts from which tubular white flowers extend. Flowers fade more quickly in full sun, but plants can be pruned to keep them in bloom and to thicken them up.

Spider Plant or Airplane Plant
Chlorophytum comosum
Nearly full sun to moderately low light

One of the most popular hanging basket plants, airplane plants are also used as a bedding plant groundcover; cold-hardy even in the Panhandle. It makes a sprawling clump of long, narrow, arching, grass-like leaves, either solid green or variegated. It's two- or three-foot flowering stems, also arching up and then back downward, will be covered with half-inch white flowers, resulting in miniature plantlets, each of which can be cut off and quickly rooted into a new plant.

187

Wandering Jew
Tradescantia fluminensis
Part shade or shade

There are several common trailing plants in this group, all of which have rapidly-growing, juicy stems that snap off easily (but are also easy to root), covered with generally pointy-oval leaves. The plants come in plain green or variegated with white stripes, yellow stripes, or leaves banded in white and pale lavender. 'Aurea' has bright yellow-green foliage. Three-petaled white flowers are not very showy.

Wax Plant
Hoya carnosa
Part shade or shade

The trailing vine, which can grow several yards long in a hanging basket, has thick, rigid leaves to about four inches long and half as wide, and produces big, round clusters of pinkish white flowers that are fragrant and appear to be made of wax. Can be trained on a pillar. 'Variegata' has white leaf edges with a touch of pink; 'Exotica' has yellow and pink variegation. The "Hindu rope" ('Krinkle Kurl' or 'Compacta') has tightly curled leaves.

Weeping Fig
Ficus benjamina
Sun, part sun, part shade

Very popular potted plant for large areas indoors or out, or in the ground in Central and South Florida. Fast-growing with small pointed oval leaves, it often sheds foliage when grown in direct air-conditioner drafts or moved suddenly to a new location, but it quickly recovers. Cultivars include a cleanly variegated form. My favorite close relative is *Ficus bennendijkii* with long, narrow, willow-like leaves that are less prone to shedding.

Cacti and Succulents

Some tropical plants endure dry spells by storing water in their swollen stems or leaves. Some have very small leaves during wet seasons, which shed during dry spells. All should be grown in very well-drained, sandy or gravelly soils or in raised beds or pots. Light feedings during the most active growing season, and occasional deep soakings, plus a good amount of sunlight, are all these plants need to thrive. Many of the following plants can be grown outdoors in all parts of Florida; however, many are grown in containers just to control the amount of water they get, and to bring them in during a sudden deep freeze in northern counties.

Burn Plant
Aloe vera
Sun, part sun, part shade

Rosettes of narrow, upright leaves with short spines on the edges, thick and succulent (sap has long been used medicinally to soothe cuts and burns). Leaves are up to a foot long. Flowers are yellow and produced on a dense spike up to three feet long. Frost tender. There are many different aloes, including the giant multi-trunk tree aloe (A. *arborescens*) that gets to ten feet tall and is winter hardy in most of Florida.

Carrion Cactus or Starfish Cactus
Stapelia species
Sun or part sun

This cactus-like plant (not a true cactus) grows as a spreading clump of jointed, four-sided stems six to nine inches long. It is very drought tolerant. When it flowers, the large, unusual, pointed buds open into sprawling, five-pointed flat stars surrounding a circular fleshy disk. Depending on the species, flowers are yellowish or purplish with darker spots or bars. They smell like dead meat, as a way to attract pollinating flies.

Crown of Thorns
Euphorbia milii var. *splendens*
Part sun or part shade

Frost-sensitive shrub with slender, upright branches armed with many sharp spines; can be trained as an espalier. Upper stems have thin, rounded leaves and are fairly continuously topped with loose clustered pairs of small flowers in red, orange, yellow, or pink. The stems root readily. Its milky sap is characteristic of all *Euphorbia* species.

Devil's Backbone
Pedilanthus tithymaloides ssp. *smallii*
Full sun to light shade

In the tropics, this densely stemmed tropical shrub is grown even in cemeteries. It can get to waist high or taller, and three feet across, in frost-free parts of Florida. Sometimes called "red bird cactus" because its red flowers resemble birds in silhouette, this milky-sap succulent has branched, crooked stems, which zigzag at each leaf joint; leaves can be plain green or green-and-white variegated with a touch of pink in sunny gardens.

Donkey Tail or Burro Tail
Sedum morganianum
Part shade or shade

Popular hanging basket or cascading container plant with many hanging "tails" to four feet or more long, densely matted with overlapping thick, gray-green fleshy leaves. Red flowers are near the bottom tips of branches, but are rarely produced. Very easy to root and start new plants. Protect from gusty winds outdoors (which knock the leaves off) or bring indoors and place near a sunny window.

Hens and Chicks
Sempervivum tectorum
Sun or part sun

This easy-to-share potted plant or rock garden addition forms a dense mat of short stems ending in tight rosettes up to four or five inches across of red-brown leaves with bristly tips. Flowers are not very showy but the plants themselves are very interesting, and need watering only to keep them from shriveling up.

Jade Plant
Crassula ovata
Sun, part sun, part shade

It is said that you should only water this thick-trunked shrub with fat, thumb-size leaves every twenty-five years or so, or it will go dormant. But it will resume growth after the first rain. This superb container specimen is among the easiest tropical plants to grow, unless you over-water it. Flowers are clustered and star-shaped. There are variegated or red-tinged forms, including 'Tricolor' with green, white, and pink foliage.

Kalanchoe
Kalanchoe blossfeldiana
Sun or part sun

Properly pronounced KA-lan-CO-eh, this common "supermarket florist" plant has large, flat, rounded leaves that are sometimes thinly edged with red. In the late winter or spring, airy stems hold large clusters of small but cheerful bright red, orange, yellow, pink, or salmon flowers. 'Pumila' and 'Vulcan' are dwarf seed-grown selections used as bedding plants. Plants are also very easy to root and spread around.

Mother of Thousands
Kalanchoe daigremontiana
Sun or part sun

One of the most unusual plants commonly passed around among gardeners. This fleshy-leaf succulent, known also as maternity plant, has long, arrowhead-shaped leaves that are spotted with purple, and many toothed notches along the edges in which small plantlets are produced—complete with leaves and roots of their own—which fall off and sprout nearly everywhere.

Night Blooming Cereus
Hylocereus and *Selenicereus* species
Part sun or part shade

These popular passalong plants have several forms—some with long, almost vine-like three-ribbed leaves, others with long, flat, toothed leaves more like jagged swords. Both produce big fat buds that open only at night into large, exotic, white or pinkish flowers that are sweetly scented, but are completely spent by the next morning. Plants can bloom all summer. Occasional fruits are edible and sweet.

Pencil Cactus
Euphorbia tirucalli
Full sun to bright indirect light

This plant is sometimes called "milk bush" because of its thick shrubby growth and milky sap. So many gardeners have gotten their "start" of this tall, twiggy oddity from other gardeners that it may be the most passed-around potted plant in the country. Not a cactus at all (it's in the same family as poinsettia), it is named for its thin, cylindrical stems, which look like lots of green pencils stacked end-to-end. The green stems are thornless and usually leafless.

Ponytail Palm

Beaucrnea recurvata

Part sun

I have had one of these Mexican yucca relatives in the same pot for nearly twenty-five years, with at most a monthly soaking. It can take short temperature dips into the teens. It is best kept in a pot or planted in very well-drained sandy soil so excess rainfall won't cause soft spots to develop on its large bulbous base. The topknot of foliage can be a fountain of narrow leaves that hang down three feet or more.

Snake Plant

Sansevieria trifasciata

Very bright light to very low light

Talk about tough—this succulent from Africa can grow in an ashtray on top of the TV! And go months without water. I have collected many different kinds of *Sansevieria* (sans-see-VAIR-ee-uh), also called mother-in-law's tongue; some are still alive after minimal care for over thirty years in the same pots. Rhizome-like runner stems can be divided, or allowed to spread into a groundcover that can actually be hard to get rid of. This is a *very* tough plant.

Soap Aloe

Aloe saponaria

Sun

I have seen this succulent plant growing around an abandoned mobile home in the Panhandle, and in hollows carved into coral south of Miami. Its foot-wide flattened rosettes of fleshy leaves spotted with white are interesting enough, but when topped with two-and-a-half-foot sprays of shrimp pink, red, orange, or yellow flowers it is really exotic. It often spreads into fair-size colonies under the worst hot, dry conditions.

Help! I'm a Garden Nerd!

Ever have a sprig of rosemary soaking in a water glass beside the sink, left over from a nice meal out on the town the evening before? Anyone who brings food home to root has a problem, possibly an addiction.

There should be a twelve-step Gardeners Anonymous program, for those who garden every day, spend family money on plants (often just because they are on sale, whether they're needed or not), and can't stay focused on anything else when driving around town. Can't you just hear it now? "Hi, I'm Felder, and I am a gardener." ("Welcome, Felder, we are glad you are here. Come back often.")

Sound close to home? Here's a simple test to see if you, too, need help:

■ Do you grow ten or more different kinds of the same plant (rose, daylily, orchid, African violet, camellia, tomato, whatever), and know their names? Extra points if they're labeled.

■ Do you subscribe to three or more garden magazines?

■ Do you keep a small shovel in your car trunk?

■ Do you buy birdseed by the fifty pound sack?

■ Do you own a $40 pair of pruning shears (bonus points for a leather scabbard)?

■ Are entire flats of flowers still sitting in the driveway because there's simply no more space to plant?

■ Have you ever willingly taken a tour of a garden by flashlight?

■ Do we need to search your purse or camera case for purloined seeds after a visit to a botanical garden?

■ Are your cuticles dirty right now?

■ Do you know the name of your county Extension Service horticulturist?

■ Do the loading guys at the local garden center know you by name?

■ And last, but not least, triple points if you would appreciate a special someone sending you a load of manure as an anniversary gift.

I'm not suggesting we gardeners should quit—though we all claim we can, any time. Maybe our motto should be One Flower at a Time. And remember, denial is a symptom!

Vines
WITH VIGOR

Vines are the most overlooked group of plants available to gardeners. Yet they are everywhere, clambering up trees in the native woods, sprawling along roadsides, cascading down hillsides and creek banks, and softening the edges of fences and arbors in every small town and country garden. There are dozens of great vines that need little or no care at all, other than occasional pruning to keep them out of our faces and off of other plants.

Technically, vines are just flexible stems that don't stop growing; they constantly get longer, reach higher, and spread into new areas. Some are multiple-branched and make good screens or groundcovers. There are annuals to be replanted every year or tender tropical plants that must be brought in every winter. Others are herbaceous perennials that leap from the ground every spring or long-lived woody landscape features that provide a year-round framework of texture for many years. Some grow so fast they can take over a porch in a few weeks or months; others seem to take forever to get established and depend on their supports to give the desired vertical effect until they catch on.

Vines and their supports lend crucial "vertical appeal" to landscapes. They provide framing, creating focal points and lifting our view from the lawn and flower beds to eye level and above. They mask bare walls to provide fast shade on the hot side of a house or hide ugly scenery. Several provide erosion control or grow in areas that are too difficult to mow or too shady for grass. They provide colorful flowers in the spring, summer, and fall; gorgeous autumn colors; and evergreen texture or accents through the winter.

Aggressive Vines

Botanical pythons such as honeysuckle and poison ivy are normally not the first—or even the last—choices for use in landscapes, but they have their places. Some gardeners and naturalists get upset over the use of "invasive exotic" plants in landscapes because they have escaped from gardens and begun to take over natural areas, sometimes displacing native plants, and becoming difficult or expensive to control. But just as the similarly invasive (but native) muscadine is often carefully placed and tended, other vine "thugs" can be controlled or converted into mannerly garden favorites. And many native plants can be "invasive" as well—a single oak tree can shade out a beautiful flower or vegetable garden.

But it is good to consider the impact of "weedy" vines on neighbors and nearby natural areas. Think twice before planting them, make sure they are in a good spot for control, and take care to keep them in bounds. When selecting overly vigorous vines, consider how far they can reach. Place them away from other plants and make sure you can at least walk all the way around them, keep an eye on errant shoots, and prune or mow what is not wanted. If you choose to grow "weedy" vines, even with great care, expect criticism—but hold up your head and go on. After all, every plant is a weed somewhere.

DON'T BE WEAK WHEN IT COMES TO MAKING AN ARBOR, PERGOLA, OR OTHER VINE SUPPORT. Vines often outgrow "store-bought" arbors, and it isn't unusual for climbing roses and wisteria to tear up wooden lattice. Use sturdy four-by-six- or six-by-six-foot posts at least ten feet high to allow for vines to grow over and hang down a bit. One of the best "fabrics" for use between heavy posts is heavy-gauge concrete reinforcing mesh, with large openings to allow vines to grow through readily.

Allamanda
Allamanda cathartica
Sun or part sun

One of the most popular summer flowering vines, this vigorous, though non-invasive, climber has cheerful flowers all season long. It is often placed in the garden annually as an accent on fences, gates, or mailboxes.

FLOWER: Flared trumpets of bright buttery yellow are only three inches long but five inches wide, blooming from spring to fall in warm weather.

PLANT: Handsome, leathery, pointy-oval leaves grow on a semi-twining vine up to forty or more feet long, which needs support. Tips can be pinched out to keep plants more compact; it can even be used as a small shrub or hedge.

INTERESTING KINDS: 'Flore Pleno' has double flowers; 'Hendersonii' has exceptionally large flowers of orange-yellow. 'Chocolate Swirl' and the purple 'Cherries Jubilee' are very popular.

American Wisteria
Wisteria frutescens
Sun or part sun

Though the traditional Chinese wisteria (*W. sinensis*) is too invasive, and generally no longer available for sale, the native wisteria is much better behaved and just as showy. It needs a sturdy, tall structure to climb on.

FLOWER: Pale lilac flowers with yellow blotches appear in dense clusters on six-inch stems that hang from the vines in the spring after leaves have begun sprouting. Blossoms are followed by three-inch velvety seedpods.

PLANT: Twining vine with shiny leaves of many leaflets, can take over small trees if not pruned after flowering in the spring.

INTERESTING KINDS: 'Amethyst Falls' has large, fragrant, pale lavender flower clusters that rival any other wisteria. 'Nivea' blooms a little earlier with white flowers.

Butterfly Pea Vine

Clitoria ternatea

Sun, part sun, part shade

This Florida native vine grows well in the sand hills, scrub, and dry woods, and brings a much-needed blue to hot summer gardens. It can begin flowering within six weeks of its seeds being soaked overnight and sown.

FLOWER: Large blue with white eye "pea" flowers to two inches long in late spring and early summer, with some appearing in late summer.

PLANT: Twining vine with leaves having three leaflets; dies to the ground in north county winters but comes back reliably.

INTERESTING KINDS: Yellow butterfly pea vine (*C. mariana*) is occasionally grown in Florida.

Bougainvillea

Bougainvillea spectabilis

Sun

Perhaps the most over-planted flowering vine in Florida, bougainvillea is by far the showiest, even in northern counties where the freeze-sensitive plant may have to be set out as an annual or grown in a pot.

FLOWER: Small white tubular flowers hidden in intensely colored papery bracts of red, orange, pink, white, and purple.

PLANT: Sprawling, cascading vine to thirty feet with scattered sharp thorns and pointed oval leaves. Must be trained onto a structure since it does not climb or twist on its own. Rampant growth in irrigated or fertilized soil; restricting roots and keeping the plant on the "dry" side will help flowering.

INTERESTING KINDS: Many named cultivars include 'Mary Palmer' with red and white flowers, purplish 'Barbara Karst', and 'Raspberry Ice' with deep red flowers and green leaves splashed with white and pink variegation.

Carolina Jessamine or Yellow Jasmine

Gelsemium sempervirens

Sun or part shade

One of the first vines to bloom in late winter, the native jessamine twists to the tops of trees and shrubs. It's a favorite vine for small arbors where evergreen screening is needed, but can tear up latticework. Prune after flowering to keep it in bounds.

FLOWER: Cheerful, medium-yellow trumpets up to two inches long are produced in great clusters in the late winter with an occasional flush of flowers in the summer and fall.

PLANT: Moderate grower to twenty or more feet, with many stems wrapping and twisting around supports. Can be a loose mounding groundcover, especially on banks. The small, pointed leaves are evergreen.

INTERESTING KINDS: 'Lemon Drop' is very fragrant, 'Butterscotch' flowers again in the fall, 'Pride of Augusta' has double flowers.

Climbing Roses

Rosa species and hybrids

Full sun

There are a few good disease-free climbing roses to cover arches, walls, and fences with beauty and scent, without a lot of trouble.

FLOWER: Loose clusters of often-fragrant pink, white, red, or yellow flowers. Some types have red fruits called "hips."

PLANT: Vining shrubs that need to be tied to supports, with usually thorny canes reaching several yards long. Prune any time to remove older or wayward canes.

INTERESTING KINDS: 'Lady Banks' is a thornless vine with dusty yellow or fragrant white flowers in the spring only; Cherokee rose has huge white flowers (state flower of Georgia); 'Climbing Old Blush' blooms with masses of medium pink; 'New Dawn' is prolific with huge pinkish-white fragrant flowers; 'Don Juan' is a hearty red climber; 'Zéphirine Dröuhin' is thornless and dark pink; 'Red Cascades' is a small nonstop red rambler.

Coral or Trumpet Honeysuckle

Lonicera sempervirens

Sun or shade

Not invasive at all, this vigorous woodland native stays put and is never a nuisance. Perfect for short trellises and lattice even in shade. Excellent for hummingbirds.

FLOWER: Clusters of orange-scarlet tubular trumpets with yellow throats, up to two inches long. Berries are bright orange and showy.

PLANT: Noninvasive and loose, to about eight feet long, the vine does not attach itself readily to structures and needs tying to get started.

INTERESTING KINDS: 'Sulphurea' has yellowish flowers; 'Superba' is bright scarlet; 'Magnifica' has large flowers, bright red on the outside and yellow on the inside; goldflame honeysuckle (*L.* × *heckrottii*) has blue-green leaves and pink buds that open into flowers that are bright coral outside and rich golden inside.

Coral Vine

Antigonon leptopus

Sun or part sun

Sometimes called "rosa de Montana" and often considered weedy, I have seen this Mexican native growing effortlessly in cemeteries all across Florida, as well as on porch railings of fine old Victorian homes. It also hides ugly chain link fences very well.

FLOWER: Lacy, arching sprays of coral pink flowers are produced continuously to create an incredibly airy effect.

PLANT: Twining, lightly branching vine sprouts from an underground tuber or seeds, and can climb twenty feet or more with bright green, arrowhead shaped leaves up to five inches long. A cold winter will kill it back to the ground, but it resprouts quickly in the spring.

INTERESTING KINDS: 'Alba' has white flowers, 'Baja Red' is deep pink, and 'Rubrum' is nearly red.

Creeping Fig
Ficus pumila
Sun or part shade

One of Florida's mainstay vines for covering brick garden and house walls, or even on the facings or risers of garden steps, this member of the fig family grows close against any surface it runs into.

FLOWER: This true fig has small oblong "fruits" which are really closed flowers. Not showy.

PLANT: The slow-growing, semi-branching vine is covered with small, heart-shaped leaves that can get up to four inches long and half as wide on mature plants. It can cover a two- or three-story wall, climbing with clinging roots that can literally take the paint off any surface. It has milky sap like other figs.

INTERESTING KINDS: 'Minima' remains small and compact; 'Variegata' has creamy yellow markings.

Cross Vine
Bignonia capreolata
Sun or part shade

Thumb-size flowers of this high-climbing native vine are very attractive to hummingbirds. Rapid growth makes the vine ideal for covering walls.

FLOWER: Fat orange buds open into two-inch trumpets with two lips, reddish orange on the outside and yellowish on the inside, produced in loose clusters in leaf joints.

PLANT: Fast-growing to fifty feet or more, usually flowering only where sunlight is. Oblong leaves are four inches long, with a pair of leaflets on both sides of leaf joints like four large butterfly wings. Grows by twining and clasping with strong tendrils that wrap or stick tightly to whatever surface they touch.

INTERESTING KINDS: Free-blooming 'Tangerine Beauty' has exceptionally bright, apricot-orange tubes; 'Shalimar Red' is a repeat bloomer with reddish flowers and yellow throats.

Cypress Vine

Ipomoea quamoclit

Full sun or very light shade

Feeling unlucky with plants? This delicate, ferny vine is so easy you might actually regret getting it started; the incredibly fast-growing annual vine can wrap around everything within reach. Pull up excess vines in the summer, and leave just enough to enjoy.

FLOWER: Bright red, flaring tubular darlings scattered profusely over the entire vine, right up until frost. One of the best butterfly and hummingbird flowers around, yet too small to be as attractive to heavy bees.

PLANT: Super-fast-growing twining vine, thick enough to make a light groundcover. Foliage is airy and ferny. Vine can overpower nearby small shrubs and escape from the garden by seed.

INTERESTING KINDS: Cardinal climber (*Ipomoea multifida*) has identical flowers, but two-inch-wide leaves instead of fernlike ones.

Evergreen Wisteria

Millettia reticulata

Sun or part shade

This 2001 Florida Plant of the Year selection is a very fine substitute for "regular" wisteria, which blooms only in the spring and can be very invasive.

FLOWER: Tight clusters of rich, purple-red, wisteria-like flowers are held upright above the foliage in summer and fall, and are very fragrant. Cut off spent flowers to promote longer blooming.

PLANT: Fast-growing vine with leaves of many shiny, leathery leaflets, is evergreen in Central and South Florida. It can easily tone down a chain link fence or other baffle between neighbors.

INTERESTING KINDS: None other than the species, but both it and the native American wisteria (*W. frutescens*) are preferred substitutes for the popular but very invasive Chinese wisteria.

Firecracker Vine
Manettia cordifolia
Sun or light shade

One of the most intense hummingbird and butterfly vines around, this small-space vine can bloom all year long except during unusually cold winters in northern counties.

FLOWER: Scarlet tubular flowers up to three inches long are waxy and sometimes flushed with yellow. They remain closed at the ends for a long time, and can be "popped" by mashing quickly, like little firecrackers.

PLANT: A thickly twisting mass of thin green vines with small pointed leaves; climbs with many branches twining around one another in thick ropes to ten or more feet high.

INTERESTING KINDS: Brazilian firecracker vine (M. *inflata* or M. *luterorubra*) has two-inch-long flowers with yellow tips that resemble candy corn.

Gourds
Lagenaria, Luffa, or *Cucurbita* species
Full sun

A friend once called gourds "vegetal white-out" for their ability to cover stuff up. These rampant growers are festooned with large ornamental fruits.

FLOWER: Loofah and small kinds of gourds have small, yellow flowers; large true gourds have big, flat, white flowers. Separate male and female flowers are produced on the same plants.

PLANT: Fast-growing vines with large leaves that climb fifteen feet or more, using strong, long tendrils to wrap around everything they touch. The lush growth of a gourd vine can shade out other plants.

INTERESTING KINDS: Loofah can be skinned and the inside used like a sponge dishrag or bath scrubber. There are also long-handled dipper, bird house, and small ornamental (many shapes and sizes and colors) types.

Hyacinth Bean
Lablab purpureus (Dolichos lablab)
Full sun

This is one traffic-stopping vine, with its attractive foliage, flowers, and beans. Easy to grow on small arbors, but never a weedy nuisance, this historic vine (grown by Thomas Jefferson) is as simple as can be.

FLOWER: Upright spikes of very attractive lavender-purple, sweet-pea-like flowers stand above the foliage, followed by flat, dark, burgundy-purple bean pods nearly three inches or so long. Seeds are black with a white edge.

PLANT: Twining summer annual vine with large, divided green leaves can easily reach the top of an arbor, but rarely ventures beyond.

INTERESTING KINDS: 'Purple Darkness' has purple-green foliage and lavender and white flowers.

Japanese Honeysuckle
Lonicera japonica
Sun or light shade

A very attractive but seriously invasive vine that takes over hedgerows, woodlands, and azaleas, but also perfect for fast privacy and erosion control.

FLOWER: Tubular white-to-cream flowers with flaring lips have outstanding fragrance and delightful nectar beloved by hummingbirds and kids.

PLANT: Vigorous evergreen can reach twenty or more feet, and spreads to overgrow and smother nearby shrubs. Prune close to the ground every year to keep it in bounds, or train along the top of a fence where flowers and foliage can be appreciated, while you can keep an eye on the plant.

INTERESTING KINDS: 'Halliana' has very white flowers changing to yellow; 'Purpurea' has purple-tinged leaves and flowers that are maroon outside and white inside; 'Aureoreticulata' has leaves veined in gold.

Malabar Spinach
Basella rubrum
Sun or part sun

This is an old "passalong" vine, very sensitive to freezes but reseeds readily. Its leaves are harvested as the plant grows, and used as a summer spinach substitute, raw or cooked.

FLOWER: Not showy, but interesting. Tight seedpods are formed in leaf axils and are easy to save for sowing the next year; often reseeds itself in nearby warm soils.

PLANT: Slow-climbing vine to four or five feet long with thick, shiny, slick, slightly crinkled leaves. Pinching tips out of young plants encourages branching and more leaf production. Climbs by twining.

INTERESTING KINDS: There are both a solid green form and one with deep green leaves, red stems, and red leaf petioles.

Mandevilla
Mandevilla splendens
Sun or part shade

Sometimes called "pink allamanda" for its strong resemblance to that plant, mandevilla is less vigorous but no less spectacular, especially the several showy hybrids.

FLOWER: Flared trumpets in several shades of pink or white (depending on the hybrid) are three to five inches wide, blooming spring, summer, and fall.

PLANT: Twining vine to twenty feet long, usually pinched to keep it shorter and bushier. Root hardy most years even in North Florida if given a good layer of mulch over the winter.

INTERESTING KINDS: 'Alice du Pont' is the most popular pink form; 'Moonlight Parfait' has pink buds that open to white flowers with double-petaled pink centers; 'White Delight' has white flowers with yellow throats; 'Tango Twirl' flowers are double; 'Ruby Star' flowers open pink but mature to nearly magenta with a touch of yellow in the throat.

Mexican Flame Vine
Senecio confusus
Sun or part sun

When this bright-flowering vine is in blossom—which is all year in South Florida and most of the year in central counties—it is covered with butterflies. Too bad such a pretty plant has a new Latin name—*Senecio pseudogynoxyschanopodioides*—that one expert says sounds like a nasty disease!

FLOWER: Clusters of inch-wide flowers in bright reddish-orange with golden centers appear at the ends of every branch. Very showy when seen cascading over a wall or small trellis, or a column.

PLANT: Twining, eight-foot, many-branched vine with light green, somewhat fleshy, coarsely toothed leaves up to four inches wide. Comes back from the roots after a freeze.

INTERESTING KINDS: 'Sao Paulo' has deep orange flowers.

Moonflower or Moonvine
Ipomoea alba
Full sun or very light shade

One of the most magical events in a new gardener's life is watching moonflowers open at dusk. The large white flowers spring suddenly from relatively small "twists" of buds, releasing a fragrance into the evening air that all but overwhelms anyone whose nose is too close. Interesting night-flying moths are pollinators.

FLOWER: Flat white fragrant trumpets, up to six inches across, open in the evening from pointed buds shaped like swirls of soft ice cream. Very fragrant, and almost glow in the dark.

PLANT: Fast-growing, twisting vine up to twenty-five or thirty feet with large heart-shaped leaves; climbs arbors, teepees, or other supports by wrapping.

INTERESTING KINDS: None, but morning glory, sweet potato, and cypress vine are relatives.

Muscadine Grape
Vitis rotundifolia
Sun

The native muscadine grape is a weedy thug along woodland edges, but makes sweet, aromatic fruit. Modern varieties produce more heavily, ripen more evenly, and have less pungency than the wild and older varieties.

FLOWER: Tiny clusters of off-white blooms hidden in the leaves produce large golden yellow, red, or deep purple grapes in late summer; old varieties are either male or female, but hybrids are self-fruitful, with a single vine producing sixty or more pounds of berries.

PLANT: Woody vine that climbs with tendrils. Five-inch rounded leaves have small points around the edges. Train vines to drape over a single-wire arbor and prune it hard every winter.

INTERESTING KINDS: Commonly sold self-fruiting varieties include bronze 'Carlos' and purple-black 'Noble'.

Passion Vine
Passiflora species
Sun

One of the gulf fritillary butterfly's main host plants, the native members of this aggressive vine genus grow well in extremely poor soils, climbing and wrapping over everything they get close to. The flowers of both native and introduced varieties are among the most exotic, spicy-scented flowers in the garden.

FLOWER: Complex frilly disks of purple, blue, lavender, red, or white are produced non-stop, followed by oblong fleshy fruits.

PLANT: Rapidly-growing stems that twine and wrap with tendrils, to twenty, thirty, or more feet in a season. Caterpillars eat leaves but become beautiful butterflies, and the plants quickly recover.

INTERESTING KINDS: The native purple kinds are great. *P. edulis* 'Possum Purple' has delicious edible fruit. Red species are commonly available as well. Popular new cultivars include 'Lavender Lady' and the red 'Lady Margaret'.

Pelican Flower

Aristolochia species

Part sun or part shade

This 2004 Florida Plant of the Year is one of the oddest flowers you can grow—guaranteed to get comments when seen from below on a trellis or arbor!

FLOWER: Fantastic white flowers with purple-red veining and throat plus a slender dangling "tail" resemble curved pipes with flared openings. Their unpleasant odor attracts pollinating flies.

PLANT: The strong-growing vine twines to thirty feet, with heart-shaped leaves ten inches long that overlap. Root hardy in North Florida, evergreen in the south, it is a host for caterpillars of the gold rim butterfly and pipevine swallowtail.

INTERESTING KINDS: Dutchman's pipe (*A. macrophylla*) has smaller flowers but is hardy in all parts of Florida; calico flower (*A. littoralis*, pictured) has deep purple veining on creamy white flowers.

Purple Painted Trumpet Vine

Clytostoma callistegioides

Sun, part sun, part shade

A root-hardy vine that is surprisingly cold hardy in northern counties. Shoots hang down in cascades of foliage and flowers.

FLOWER: Very fragrant, lavender, light purple, or violet trumpets to three inches long and nearly as wide at the flared open ends. Flowers are produced in sprays at ends of new growth in the spring and summer, with a few clusters appearing in the fall.

PLANT: Sturdy climber that uses tendrils to clasp onto nearly any support, with dark-green, paired leaves (really two leaflets). The plant is hardy down to the lower teens, but should be pruned in late winter to keep it from taking over.

INTERESTING KINDS: Pandorea (*Pandorea jasminoides*) is a showy close relative, but not winter hardy in North Florida.

Sky Vine
Thunbergia grandiflora
Sun or light shade

Hardy in all parts of Florida, this stunning old "passalong plant" is a perennial vine that can be seen growing along rural fences outside country homes with intense blue flowers from spring to fall.

FLOWER: Light blue, bell-shaped blossoms, each three inches long, are produced in slightly drooping clusters.

PLANT: Twining rampant vine to twenty or more feet with large, triangular, heart-shaped leaves up to eight inches long that cast a fairly dense shade as they overlap, and provide a dark backdrop for the flower clusters.

INTERESTING KINDS: 'Alba' has white flowers with yellow throats, and heart-shaped leaves. Scrambling sky flower (*T. battiscombei*) is more shrubby, with dark purple-blue flowers with yellow throats.

Smilax or Greenbriar
Smilax lanceolata
Sun or dense shade

This Southeastern native vine is one of the most common evergreens in the woods and has been used for floral garlands and wreaths for many generations. In gardens it is typically trained over doorways, porches, and breezeways.

FLOWER: Very inconspicuous green clusters. Dull reddish brown berries can be somewhat attractive.

PLANT: New shoots arising from a hardy underground tuber are olive green and often thorny, and climb up to twenty or more feet with tendrils. Glossy evergreen leaves are sometimes variegated.

INTERESTING KINDS: Jackson vine (*Smilax smallii*) is favored by florists for its six-inch leaves with prominent veins that retain their color long after cutting. But "florist smilax" is really a true asparagus (*Asparagus asparagoides*).

Star or Confederate Jasmine
Trachelospermum jasminoides
Sun or light shade

One of the most popular old fragrant vines of Florida, this sturdy plant almost stands up without supports, with glossy leaves and fragrant flowers, blooming even on an arbor in the shade.

FLOWER: The display and delicious fragrance of snow-white, pinwheel-shaped blossoms begins heavily in the spring, and continues for several weeks into early summer. Good for bees, so don't plant by a door.

PLANT: Dense vine with very glossy, two- to three-inch leaves climbs by twining to thirty or more feet with even longer shoots; can be kept pruned onto a wall or smaller trellis, kept on a mailbox, or used as a dense groundcover.

INTERESTING KINDS: 'Variegatum' has creamy yellow blotches on deep green leaves.

Sweet Autumn Clematis
Clematis paniculata
Sun or light shade

Normally I would not include clematis in a list of unkillable plants, because showy hybrids need cold weather and can suffer from heat and humidity. But the native species, though not as showy with smaller flowers, are stunning as they cover an arbor or fence.

FLOWER: Very showy masses of small white flowers in the fall, with interesting seed heads afterwards.

PLANT: Attractive vines climb several yards, with dark green divided leaves. Grows by wrapping around stakes, arbors, or other plants. Can be invasive if not tended to regularly.

INTERESTING KINDS: C. *armandii* has medium-sized white flowers on super-vigorous stems that require regular pruning to keep in bounds; C. *crispa* is a native with sparse, bell-shaped, lavender flowers, not a very vigorous vine.

Trumpet Vine

Campsis radicans

Sun or light shade

This vigorous native is among the best for fast coverage and hummingbirds. Plant it where you can walk around it for maintenance, or it will take over!

FLOWER: Clusters of thumb-sized trumpets of bright orange or red, followed by large, canoe-like seedpods, five to six inches long.

PLANT: Extremely vigorous vine climbs forty or more feet long by twisting and attaching with aerial roots—even onto metal poles. Foot-long leaves hold nine or more pointed leaflets.

INTERESTING KINDS: Hybrid 'Crimson Trumpet' is deep red; 'Flava' is yellow or pale orange; Chinese trumpet creeper (*C. grandiflora* or *C. chinensis*) is not as large a vine as the native, but has slightly larger, red flowers. Hybrid 'Madame Galen' has bright orange to red flowers.

Other Good Vines:

Black-Eyed Susan Vine (*Thunbergia alata*) is root-hardy in all parts of Florida when grown in the ground. It sprouts quickly from seed into a tidy small climber or hanging basket vine, with a continuous show of striking orange, yellow, or white trumpet-shaped flowers, each with a purple-black "throat" spot.

Bleeding Heart Vine or **Glory Bower** (*Clerodendrum thomsoniae*) is one of the few flowering vines for shade. This showy plant blooms all summer and fall with white "Chinese lantern" calyxes that fade to pink and purple, with a red flower hanging from the bottom. It, along with other glory bower vines, can freeze in northern Florida.

Cape Honeysuckle (*Tecomaria capensis*) is a freeze-sensitive vine with brilliant orange, red, gold, or salmon flowers in compact clusters from fall to spring. Versatile enough for many landscape uses, even a small tree.

Chalice Vine or **Gold Cup Vine** (*Solandra maxima*) is a vigorous tropical vine, hardy only to Central Florida, with large glossy leaves and huge, five-inch-wide bowl-shaped golden flowers with reddish-brown stripes.

Chayote or **Mirliton** (*Sechium eudule*) is a fast-growing vine that makes two hundred or more edible "vegetable pears" in the fall. Plant store-bought fruits in the spring, sprouted end down, and mulch in the winter if frost kills the top vine.

Black-Eyed Susan Vine

Love in a Puff (*Cardiospermum halicacabum*), treated as an annual, is a twining summer vine that can reach ten feet or more. Small white flowers are followed by hollow, three-compartment fruits that contain hard, black, pea-sized seeds with a perfect white heart marking on each.

Orchid Vine (*Mascagnia macroptera*) climbs to twenty feet with yellow flowers followed by showy three- to four-inch seedpods that resemble butterflies; *M. lilacina* or yellow orchid vine is shrubby and flowers almost nonstop with yellow blooms, even in the shade.

Pandorea or **Bower Vine** (*Pandorea jasminoides*) has glossy leaves with many leaflets, and pink, bell-shaped flowers with darker centers; it can freeze in North Florida.

Potato Vine (*Solanum jasminoides* 'Variegata'), though a little invasive, is perfect for light shade over a small arbor or entryway, with continuous white flowers throughout the warm season.

Rangoon Creeper (*Quisqualis indica*) is fast growing to thirty feet, with drooping chains of fragrant white tubular flowers that turn rosy red with age, followed by oblong fruit.

Sandpaper Vine or **Purple Wreath Vine** (*Petrea volubilis*), named Florida Plant of the Year in 2003, grows to thirty-five feet and has five-petaled blue flowers in clusters that resemble wisteria. It will not tolerate a hard freeze in North Florida.

 **Best for Beginners:**

- *Carolina Jessamine*
- *Coral Honeysuckle*
- *Coral Vine*
- *Cypress Vine* (weedy)
- *Evergreen Wisteria*
- *Gourds*
- *Hyacinth Bean*
- *Moonflower*
- *Morning Glory*
- *Passion Vine*

Kinda Tricky:

- *Clematis*
- *Japanese Honeysuckle*
- *Muscadine Grape*
- *Tomato*
- *Trumpet Creeper*
- *Wisteria*

Scarlet Runner Bean (*Phaseolus coccineus*), an antique summer bean, climbs readily and has reddish orange flowers all summer. Very attractive on wooden teepees in a garden setting.

Tree Ivy (*Fatshedera lizei*), a perfect cross between fatsia and ivy, is an upright "semi-shrub vine" perfect for a lightly shaded spot where a vine would be too tall and a shrub would be too wide, such as along a courtyard wall or beside a pool.

Virginia Creeper (*Parthenocissus quinquefolia*) is a very hardy, rampant native vine often confused with poison ivy (they are actually in different plant families), but with five leaflets instead of three. Very good for sun or dense shade, with a hard-to-find variegated form.

Windowleaf Philodendron (*Monstera deliciosa*) is a slow-growing, freeze-sensitive philodendron relative with large pointy-oval leaves with oblong holes or "windows" between the veins.

Wisteria (*Wisteria* species), as beautiful, fragrant, and commonly planted as it is, has been discouraged for sale in Florida for its habit of taking over native plant areas. Many good cultivars may be available, but it's better to use native wisteria (*W. frutescens*) or evergreen wisteria (*Millettia reticulata*).

Rumpelstiltskin's Garden

Remember the old fable of the gnome who wove golden garments from common straw? As I wander around my little cottage garden, I realize that it is a "Rumpelstiltskin" tapestry of sorts.

Because my busy family and I relax in our garden year-round, we try to have plants for every season. Ours is a cottage garden, with a style and freedom to grow what we like, where we like, and includes something for all the senses, including taste and touch. Though I've collected rare plants during my travels around the horticulture world, my landscape's backbone is mostly "comfort plants" shared between generous gardeners over many years. Potted plants and hanging baskets are everywhere, and made from a wide variety of containers, and there are many "hard features" such as bird baths, urns, small statuary, whimsical "yard art", and found objects (rocks, driftwood, etc.).

To outsiders, there is no apparent design, but it has a definite personal layout—best viewed inside-out (from the house, not the street). Our garden is much more than just its plants; the ever-changing scenery is screened from prying

eyes of passing joggers with lattice-like fencing, painted teal and pastels to help give a glow of color without being garish. We placed a few comfortable chairs on roomy decks, and connected each "people space" with meandering paths. There's a waterfall to soothe city sounds, and a large iron bowl on one deck for tending crackling wood fires on chilly evenings.

Having a garden like this increases the likelihood of year-round enjoyment with less work. And just as our "garden of welcome" is alive with birds and other wildlife that delight us with colorful motion and busy chatter, we invite friends over to relax beside our water garden and fire pit. Soon they feel comfortable enough to share stories and laughter, which enriches our lives more. Rumplestiltskin would be proud.

WONDERFUL
Water Plants

Anyone who has ever rooted a sweet potato, avocado seed, or philodendron cutting in a glass jar in the kitchen window—or even grown fungus in a cup of coffee—pretty much has all the basics of water gardening figured out. Everything else—adding a goldfish to the bowl, or hooking up in a little splashy fountain or waterfall—is finesse.

We're not getting into "how to make a water garden" here. There are too many other great resources for that. This is mostly a run-down on some of the best aquatic plants for Florida water and bog gardens. Still, there are some basic guidelines you should follow for a simple water garden:

- Anything that holds water will work—a preformed water garden tub, plastic-lined half whiskey barrel, kid's wading pool, aluminum foot tub, old bathtub, five-gallon paint bucket, etc.
- Maintain the water level by replacing what evaporates during hot spells.
- Drain and clean the pond at least once a year to remove sunken debris that can build up and cause water quality problems.
- Mosquitoes require still water to breed, and will be a problem unless you have fish, or moving water (a waterfall or fountain), or use natural pesticide "mosquito dunks" to kill larvae safely.
- You do not need to have fish in a water garden; if you do have them, don't overfeed them!
- If your water stays murky or green, plant a shade tree over the pond, or have two-thirds or more of the water surface covered with plants. A filter can help, as can "quick fix" algaecides.
- **CAUTION:** If you use a water pump, make sure it is plugged into a "ground fault interrupter" electric outlet like those found in bathrooms, that will pop out its button-like fuse if you run into trouble with electricity; it is cheap, and can save your life.

Aquatic plants come in three basic categories: floating, submerged, and marginal (shallow water, mud, or bog plants). Each has a wide range of foliage and flower types; some are tall and narrow, some are frilly or rounded, and some are very low-growing like groundcovers. One VERY important note on invasive species: Some popular aquatic plants, especially water hyacinth and water lettuce, have escaped into natural waterways and caused serious ecological and economic problems. These two in particular should not be planted in Florida! Two

others to avoid, both marginal or wetland plants, are taro (*Colocasia*, a type of elephant's ear) and yellow flags iris (*Iris pseudacorus*). Even some native plants can be very invasive, especially dwarf cattails, lizard tail, thalia, and horsetail. Use them with caution, and be prepared to divide them often!

Here are a few general guidelines for planting and maintaining aquatic plants:

- Most water garden plants need at least half a day of sunshine to grow well and bloom.
- Plant in wide containers with gravel in the bottom, especially shallow bog plants that need to be bottom heavy so they won't tip over in sudden gusts of wind.
- Plant just like ordinary potted garden perennials, only in good garden soil, not potting soil.
- Cover the top of the soil with at least two inches of gravel, sand, or other heavy "mulch" to keep the soil in, especially in a water garden that has fish.
- Fertilize annually with pellets made just for water garden plants, or with slow-release Osmocote.

- In northern and some central counties, frost may damage the foliage of some plants; simply cut off the frost-damaged foliage.
- Divide water garden plants in the winter or as needed.

Floating Plants

Free-floating kinds of plants have very small or furry roots that hang beneath masses of foliage that spread over the surface of the water. Their leaves are usually very attractive, waxy, and naturally water repellent. Most provide important food for fish, and can cover the water surface to help keep algae down. Many are so fast spreading they have to be thinned regularly to keep them from covering the water completely. These are not covered in this book because most are so weedy and aggressive they will take over Florida water gardens.

ALAN SHAPIRO, owner of Grandiflora Wholesale Nursery near Gainesville, planted a little water lettuce in his huge irrigation pond to clear algae from the water, and within just a few months he had a solid mass of what seemed like a million plants spread completely over the entire pond. He was amazed, considereing how a single plant sells for around five bucks in aquatic shops up North!

Submerged Plants

Submerged plants are planted in pots of garden dirt (just like garden plants) that are sunk beneath the water, with six inches to two feet of water above their soil to give long stems and wide leaves room to grow up and float. Plant in "real dirt" because organic matter in potting soil will float away or rot and cause root problems. Every spring poke water garden plant food into the soil.

Arrowhead (*Sagittaria latifolia*) is a native perennial submerged plant that gets up to three feet tall with glossy, dark green leaves in narrow triangular arrowhead shapes. It is very hardy and evergreen even in North Florida.

Four-Leaf Water Clover (*Marsilea lutea*) is a favorite submerged plant that grows best in shallow water, with spreading, floating, four-petaled leaves with a distinctive pattern of green, yellow, and red. M. *quadrifolia* holds its solid green leaves above the water.

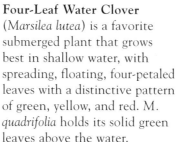

Arrowhead

Four-Leaf Water Clover

Lotus (*Nelumbo* species) is one of the surprises of the water garden—the submerged plants, which need at least six or eight inches of water above its soil, send up huge, waxy green dinner-plate shaped leaves over a foot across, held above the water on slender stalks. The flowers are as beautiful as any water lily, in reds, pinks, and yellows, and very interesting seed pods are popular for dried arrangements. The plant is winter hardy into Canada.

Lotus

Parrot's Feather

Parrot's Feather (*Myriophyllum aquaticum*) is a very invasive but popular aquarium and water garden plant that gets its name from the feather-like appearance of its green leaves, which grow in whorls around long stems both under and above the water surface. A "nicer" dwarf form with tighter leaves and brilliant red stems is available and easier to control. **Note:** The similar but looser-leaved "Eurasian water milfoil" (M. *spicatum*) is prohibited in Florida as a serious invasive exotic.

Water Lilies

Water Lilies (*Nymphaea* species) are almost always the focal point of the water garden with their beautiful, round, glossy leaves, six to eight inches or more across. They need at least six, but no more than eighteen, inches of water above the plants to give leaves room to spread out on the surface. The dense foliage provides much-needed shade to keep out algae, and cover for fish. Water lilies—of which there are many dozens of wonderful varieties available—flower mostly in the day, though there are some tropical night-flowering kinds; their blossoms are fist-sized, single or double and daisy-like, and sometimes fragrant. Tropical kinds can be left outside even along the Gulf Coast.

Nymphoides species are similar to water lilies, with small, heart-shaped leaves and lots of one- or two-inch-wide, fringed, snowflake-like flowers.

Bog Plants

Often called "marginal" because they grow naturally between land and water, bog plants are usually tall and flowering. Since they grow in shallow water, they will need to be set atop bricks or plastic "milk crates" so the top of the soil is at or just below the water surface. It is fine to plant bog plants in a mixture of soil and potting soil. Instead of growing bog plants directly in the water garden, consider planting them just outside where they look like they are in the water, complementing the scene without taking up precious water garden space. Place taller plants towards the back of your view, and smaller, softer-textured ones closer to the water garden to help conceal its edges.

On the following pages are a few very commonly grown bog beauties; other water-tolerant plants include canna, scarlet hibiscus, bald cypress, blue flags iris, cordgrass, sweetbay magnolia, miscanthus grass, ruellia, cardinal flower, butterfly ginger, spiderwort, wedelia, narrow-leaf sunflower, and elephant's ear.

Alligator Flag (*Thalia geniculata*) is an upright native "ditch" plant with three- or four-foot stems topped with narrow, canna-like leaves, each one cradling an erect stem of very showy blue or pink flowers from spring to fall. It can be seen growing in low areas along most Florida roadsides.

Bull Rush (*Scirpus lacustris*) is a bog plant for the edge of big ponds. The large clump-forming plant gets up to five feet tall, producing an explosion of dark green, very narrow needle-like leaves with small eruptions of brown "flowers" appearing near the ends. Variegated forms are available.

Alligator Flag

Bull Rush

Common Rush (*Juncus effusus*) is a much smaller bog plant than bull rush, and forms less of a clump. My favorite is the dwarf 'Spiralis' with its very interesting, tight corkscrew foliage.

Calla

Chameleon Plant (*Houttuynia cordata* 'Tricolor' or 'Variegata') is a fast-spreading groundcover with heart-shaped leaves, usually variegated with green, yellow, white, and pinkish red, and small white flowers. Once you plant this somewhat invasive plant, you may have it for good.

Calla (*Zantedeschia aethiopica*) is the common green-foliage plant seen in older gardens where soils are moist. Its canna-like leaves can reach over three feet tall, with slightly taller stalks of exotic, cutting-quality flowers made of pure white spathes surrounding a yellow central spadix. Other species have spotted or golden foliage and pink, lavender, purple, or yellow flowers.

Chameleon Plant

Dwarf Cattail (*Typha minima*) is much more manageable than "regular" cattails, which are native plants that can get up to six or more feet tall and completely take over wet areas. Dwarf cattail is a bog plant that only gets two or so feet tall with very narrow, blue-green foliage and one-inch, oblong cattails that look like miniature hot dogs on skewers.

Dwarf Cattail

Horsetail (*Equisetum hyemale*) can be a real thug in moist soil, but can be contained easily in pots in a water garden. Its colonies have many upright, three- or four-foot-tall stems that are dark green, hollow, jointed, and leafless, with a small club-like "flower" cone at the tips. It is an excellent native evergreen that mosquito-eating dragonflies love to perch on.

Horsetail

Lizzard Tail

Lizard Tail (*Saururus cernuus*) is a fast-spreading native bog plant that grows in small colonies from underground runners. Its narrow, heart-shaped leaves are topped with curved, bottlebrush-like white flower spikes. It can become a pest in wet areas, so be prepared to dig and share with others.

Papyrus (*Cyperus papyrus*) is a bog plant with many tall, stiff, triangular (in cross-section) stems topped with attractive "mop heads" of needle-like foliage. The heavy clusters cause stems to weep gracefully. Use as a strong accent or specimen. Dwarf papyrus (*C. haspan*) is smaller with golden-green flowers that turn rusty bronze in the late summer.

Papyrus

Pickerel Rush

Pickerel Rush (*Pontederia cordata*) is an upright native bog plant with three- or four- foot stems topped with narrow, canna-like leaves, and erect stems with very showy blue flowers from spring to fall. It grows well with horsetail and parrot's feather.

Pitcher Plant

Pitcher Plant (*Sarracenia* species) is one of the oddest plants on earth—yet it is native to Florida's southern counties, where it colonizes in low-fertility, wet bogs. There are many varieties, with the narrow, hooded, hollow, pitcher-like leaf, which traps and drowns insects as a food source, ranging from six inches to nearly two feet tall; they can be green, yellow, or red, and usually have distinct vein markings. The flowers hang upside down on narrow stalks beside the pitcher leaves.

String Lily (*Crinum americanum*) is a bold-textured native bulb with strap-like leaves and two-foot flower stalks topped with clusters of large, fragrant white flowers with very narrow petals. It is closely related to the common "swamp spider lily" (*Hymenocallis* species) that has a bit of white fabric connecting the flower petals.

Swamp Mallow

Swamp Mallow (*Hibiscus moscheutos*) is an herbaceous native perennial with white or pink flowers up to six or more inches across in midsummer and early fall. It is a host plant for some native butterflies, and sometimes has caterpillars which birds love to catch and eat.

Umbrella Sedge

Umbrella Sedge (*Cyperus alternifolia*) is a very popular marginal plant, often grown outdoors as a "regular" garden plant. It is similar to papyrus, but with umbrella-like foliage atop stiff stems. It provides a spreading, upright accent, and its roots can be a great natural filter for pond water. 'Gracilis' is a smaller, more erect, narrow-leaved variety. **Note:** It is on the "invasive plant" list.

THERE IS AN EASY TRICK to digging a water garden that uses a lot less effort than is illustrated in most "how-to" water garden manuals. Build a simple frame of pressure-treated wood (like a sandbox) in whatever shape you want, set it where the water garden should be, and level it up. Then dig out the soil inside the box, piling it up to the outside of the box. Instead of digging a "whole" hole, you will have dug only half a hole, but the combination partly-sunk, partly-raised area will have the depth you want or need, and won't wash out during heavy rains. Line the hole with pond liner, lapped over and tacked onto the top of the wood frame, and cover the edge with a board or flagstones to keep it neat.

Green Thumb is Official

Finally, the "green thumb" has been officially declared a type of intelligence! As a horticulturist, I was taught that it's all about positive human qualities such as the ability to be observant, pay attention to detail, plan ahead, and follow through on projects. But you know there's just gotta be something different, if not outright special, about folks who seem to be blessed with an unfair advantage in the natural world.

At last, Harvard professor Howard Gardner proved his "Theory of Multiple Intelligences" by finding regions of the brain that "light up" when certain abilities are practiced. In addition to the most widely accepted logical-mathematical, musical, and language-oriented "linguistics" aptitudes, he also found evidence of six other types of intelligences.

The one that most applies to the kind of gardener who can root and grow a splinter off a fencepost is called *naturalist* aptitude; simply put, people with naturalist intelligence have the ability to identify and classify patterns in nature, and make predictions based on seemingly random events.

Naturalists are very comfortable outdoors; they are constantly aware of their surroundings, looking around as they drive, watching weeds and hawks, and braking for butterflies. They observe, touch, and compare even "yucky" things, and often collect stuff—shells, rocks, and flowers. They can "just tell" when to plant, when to harvest, when to repot.

They also manipulate things to see what happens; ever-curious plant hybridizers fall heavily into the naturalist group, as do "giant tomato" or "perfect lawn" gardeners. So do wildflower enthusiasts, bonsai artists, birdwatchers, and garden teachers, especially those whose naturalist leanings are coupled with strong interpersonal and linguistic abilities.

Any of this apply to you? Mix in doses of other intelligences, and it's no wonder gardeners have such different approaches, and levels of success and satisfaction. We may not all be smart in the decisions we make—but a Harvard professor has proven that we can sure be intelligent about how we garden!

Beautiful But Bad Weeds

"Never buy those plants which you suspect are non-native." This harsh statement is included on a government-sponsored poster of invasive foreign plants sent to school children all over Florida. It comes across as knee-jerk and isolationist, but makes the point that some plants should not be grown in this environmentally super-sensitive state. Invasive plants are often the weedy bane of most gardeners' lives. But we keep pulling, chopping or spraying, like bailing out a leaky boat, and mulching to prevent more.

Exotic or non-native plants are not "bad"—they just aren't from around here. Many are fantastic in our landscapes and gardens, providing color, texture, fragrance, fruit, and many other benefits without causing any real problems. A large number, however, require extra water or fertilizer to grow well in the local climate, or attract unwanted pests. Some can easily "escape" the garden by seed or other methods, and quickly take over surrounding areas and even disrupt natural ecosystems; the sale and even growing of some of these have been banned outright by local, state, or federal agencies.

Some native plants can be just as invasive as imported "exotic" plants. Still, the Florida Exotic Pest Council brings pressure on nurserymen and landscapers to not use certain non-native plants. It places them in categories, according to how much damage or how big a threat they are to the environment.

Really Bad or So-So Bad

Category I invasive plants as those truly disruptive plants that are actually altering native plant communities by displacing native species, changing community structures or ecological functions, or hybridizing with native plants. Some of the plants on this list are prohibited by the federal government from being planted.

Category II plants are those that "have increased in abundance or frequency but have not yet altered Florida plant communities to the extent shown by Category I species." Some are banned in certain areas by local government agencies, but none are banned by the state, and continue to be planted by the gardening public.

The Category II invasive exotics list, by the way, includes such widely loved plants as wax begonia, pothos, Chinese fan palm, and snake plant. But, oddly enough, it does not include the over-planted, water and pesticide hungry, ecologically-disruptive turfgrasses! For more information on exotic plants that have become real pests in Florida, contact the Florida Exotic Pest Council (www.fleppc.org), or pick up literature at any county Extension Service office.

Banned or Not-Recommended Invasive Plants

The following Category I plants are banned by the government, or otherwise on my NOT RECOMMENDED list. Some I love dearly for their beauty and usefulness, and they are put on this list with great reluctance. But the truth is, in general they are no longer offered for sale anyway:

- Ardisia (*Ardisia elliptica*)
- Australian Pine (*Casuarina equisetifolia*)
- Beach Naupaka (*Scaevola sericea*)
- Brazilian Pepper (*Schinus terebinthifolius*)
- Chinese Tallow (*Sapium sebiferum*)
- Cogon Grass (*Imperata cylindrica*)
- Ear-leaf Acacia (*Acacia auriculiformis*)
- Gold Coast Jasmine (*Jasminum dichotomum*)
- Japanese Climbing Fern (*Lygodium japonicum*)
- Kudzu (*Peuraria montana*)
- Laurel Fig (*Ficus microcarpa*)
- Melaleuca (*Melateu quiquenervia*)
- Multiflora Rose (*Rosa multiflora*)
- Potato Vine (*Dioscorea bulbifera* and other species)
- Taro (*Colocasia esculenta*)
- Water Hyacinth (*Eichhornia crassipes*)
- Water Lettuce (*Pistia stratiotes*)
- Wisteria (*Wisteria floribunda, W. sinensis*)

Natives Can Be Thugs, Too

There are many good reasons for using certain native plants in your landscape, including their being well-adapted to our soil and climate, their importance as food and shelter for native wildlife, their beauty, and the way they help create an overall "sense of place" that continues to remind us why this state is named after its floral beauty. The Association of Florida Native Nurseries is your very best source for information on selecting, locating, and using native plants. For members near you, contact them at www.afnn.org or the Florida Native Plant Society (www.fnps.org).

Still, some natives are just plain troublesome in the landscape—they want to revert our gardens to a natural, jungle-, or dune-like condition. I'd like to see a poster showing "Invasive Natives"—naturally-occurring plants that can easily "get away" from a gardener, including muscadine grape, some ferns, spotted horsemint, cherry laurel, river oats, Carolina jessamine, cross vine, trumpet creeper, saw palmetto, sumac, dichondra, narrowleaf sunflower, Mexican primrose, passion flower, and sweet autumn clematis. Not to mention poison ivy and dodder. Instead, let me just remind you to be careful when selecting ANY potentially weedy plant, native or not . . .

Use These with Great Caution

I still insist that you should be able to grow and enjoy the following plants, even though their offspring can become bullies in your neighbor's gardens. Though they are on the university's "official unofficial" list of plants to avoid, they are not outright banned by any state agency. Many are widely available for sale; however, I recommend them only with a strongly worded PLANT WITH CARE warning:

- Arrowhead Vine (*Syngonium podophyllum*)
- Asparagus Fern (*Asparagus densiflorus* Sprengeri Group
- Bamboo (running kinds, especially *Phyllostachys* species)
- Bauhinia (*Bauhinia variegata*)
- Castor Bean (*Ricinus communis*, seeds are toxic!)
- Chinaberry (*Melia azedarach*)
- Chinese Privet (*Ligustrum sinense*)
- Coral Ardisia (*Ardisia crenata*)
- Japanese Honeysuckle (*Lonicera japonica*)
- Lantana (*Lantana aculeata*, plant seedless cultivars only)
- Mimosa (*Albizia julibrissin*)
- Nandina (*Nandina domestica*, avoid fruiting kinds)
- Parrot's Feather (*Myriophyllum aquaticum*)
- Princess Tree (*Paulownia tomentosa*)
- Purple Loosestrife (*Lythrum salicaria*)
- Ruellia (*Ruellia brittoniana*)
- Scaevola (*Scaevola sericea*)
- Schefflera (*Schefflera actinophylla*, not legal to plant in Dade County)
- Strawberry Gava (*Pisidium cattleianum*)
- Striped Cane (*Arundo donax* 'Variegata')
- Surinam Cherry (*Eugenia uniflora*)
- Sword Fern (*Nephrolepsis cordifolia*)
- Tall Oyster Plant (*Tradescantia spathacea*)
- Umbrella Sedge (*Cyperus alternifolia*)
- Wedelia (*Wedelia trilobata*)
- White Flowering Wandering Jew (*Tradescantia albiflora*)
- Yellow Flag Iris (*Iris pseudcacorus*)
- Last, but not least: Wide expanses of turfgrass

Bibliography

Instead of the usual bibliography, let me just tell you that I cross-referenced TONS of great books on gardening in Florida and the Southeast. In them I found snippets of information that I missed on my many visits to Florida gardens, and clarification of fine details. But mostly I used them to make sure I didn't overlook many cool plants.

I pored over details, triple-checked them, and ran them by Florida horticulturists, nurserymen, Master Gardeners, and other gardeners. I also spent many hours on Internet "chat rooms" populated by Florida gardeners—especially after hurricanes—to see what survived and what didn't.

So, on top of personal scratching and sniffing, I took advantage of many sources of information directly related to growing tough plants in the Sunshine State.

Take a close look at the photo, which is of a shelf in my personal library, and see if there are some of your favorite references there as well.

Just remember, no book is as good as getting down and dirty in your own garden.

Photo Credits

Thomas Eltzroth: 23, 25a, 27b, 29ab, 30a, 32ab, 33a, 37b, 39b, 40ab, 41a, 51b, 54a, 55a, 56a, 57b, 58b, 59ab, 65b, 66d, 67b, 75a, 77, 78ab, 79b, 88a, 90a, 91ab, 93ab, 94b, 95a, 100b, 101b, 102a, 103a, 109a, 110a, 113ab, 114b, 115a, 116a, 117b, 119a, 120b, 122a, 123ab, 124, 125b, 127, 130ab, 132ab, 134ab, 135a, 137a, 138a, 140ab, 141b, 142ab, 143a, 144a, 145b, 147, 148a, 149ab, 151ab, 153ab, 158b, 159a, 160ab, 161a, 162a, 163a, 164a, 165a, 166a, 167b, 168a, 170, 171, 173, 177, 180b, 182ab, 183a, 184c, 185ab, 186ab, 187bc, 191bc, 198, 199bc, 200a, 203a, 204b, 206b, 208b, 211b, 212b, 219c, 220b, 222ab, 223ac, 224a, 225a

Felder Rushing: 9, 10, 13, 14, 15, 18, 20, 24, 26a, 28a, 30b, 31b, 33b, 35a, 38ab, 44, 46, 50a, 53, 55b, 60, 63a, 64b, 66b, 68, 73ab, 74ab, 80ab, 81ab, 84, 86, 87, 92a, 96, 99, 102b, 103b, 104ab, 105, 110b, 111b, 112b, 114a, 120a, 121a, 125a, 126, 128, 131b, 133ab, 136b, 137b, 148b, 150b, 154, 156, 159b, 162b, 163b, 166b, 169b, 174, 179, 180ac, 181ab, 183b, 187a, 188ab, 189ab, 190bc, 191a, 192abc, 193abc, 194, 196, 199a, 204a, 206a, 207b, 209a, 210ab, 214, 217, 218, 219b, 221ab, 222c, 223b, 224b, 225b, 226

Jerry Pavia: 22, 25b, 26b, 27a, 28b, 31a, 34b, 35b, 36ab, 37a, 39a, 41b, 42, 43, 49a, 50b, 51a, 52, 64d, 69, 75b, 76b, 82a, 85, 88b, 107a, 108b, 109b, 111a, 112a, 115b, 117a, 118a, 119b, 121b, 122b, 135b, 138b, 143b, 144b, 145a, 146, 152, 164b, 165b, 172, 190a, 198b, 200b, 201a, 202a, 205a, 207a, 212a

Liz Ball and Rick Ray: 34a, 47, 48b, 65c, 76a, 79a, 101a, 106b, 107b, 136a, 141ac, 158a, 197, 201b, 220a

William Adams: 54b, 66a, 72b, 82b, 106a, 108a, 118b, 169a, 170b, 182c, 184b

Lorenzo Gunn: 90b, 131a, 183c, 188c, 209b, 211a

Pam Harper: 92b, 139, 167a, 184a, 202b

Michael Dirr: 56b, 57a, 161b

Charles Mann: 49b, 65d, 205b

Bruce Holst: 63b, 89a

Stephen Pategas: 64a, 67a, 168b, 150a, 203

Dan Gill: 72a

Gerard Krewer: 208a

Kirsten Llamas: 48a

Judy Mielke: 89b

Greg Speichert: 219a

Forest and Kim Starr, USGS: 65a

Georgia Tasker: 58a

Mark Turner: 64c

Peter Loewer: 66c

Key: photos are lettered from top to bottom of page, left to right

Index

Meet the Author

Felder Rushing is a 10th-generation Southern gardener whose quirky, overstuffed cottage garden has been featured in many magazines, including *Southern Living, Garden Design, Landscape Architecture, House and Garden,* the *New York Times,* and *Better Homes and Gardens.*

In addition to many years of in-depth (what he calls "scratch-and-sniff") studies of both home and public gardens in Florida and the rest of the South, and thousands of lectures—well over a hundred a year, including dozens in every corner of Florida, working with university and industry professionals, and garden clubs and plant societies—Felder has studied in gardens around the world during numerous trips to Europe, South America, and tropical Africa. He holds two horticulture degrees and works very closely with Extension Service consumer horticulturists, often conducting advanced Master Gardener training.

He writes twice-weekly garden columns, and his live, call-in radio program broadcast on National Public Radio affiliates gets calls from gardeners in five states. He has appeared on HGTV, Educational TV, the Discovery Channel, and hosted a series shown in twelve states. Hundreds of his articles and photographs have been in over two dozen national magazines, including *National Geographic, Fine Gardening, Organic Gardening, National Wildflower Journal, Country Living Gardener,* and many others. Once a contributing editor for *Garden Design* magazine, and one of only six members of *Southern Living* magazine's garden advisory board, he currently serves as contributing editor of *Horticulture* magazine.

Felder's fourteen garden books include the award-winning *Passalong Plants,* named the "best written" garden book in the country by the Garden Writers Association, and *Tough Plants for Southern Gardens.* He is also a national board member of the American Horticultural Society.

Believing that too many of his fellow horticulturists complicate things unnecessarily, Felder says that "We are daunted, not dumb." He has spent a lifetime trying to make gardening as easy as it is fun.